INDIAN WOMEN WRITERS IN ENGLISH

INDIAN WOMEN WRITERS IN ENGLISH

(A Study of Nergis Dalal)

P.G. Javalgi

ANMOL PUBLICATIONS PVT. LTD.
NEW DELHI - 110 002 (INDIA)

ANMOL PUBLICATIONS PVT. LTD.
H.O.: 4374/4B, Ansari Road, Darya Ganj,
New Delhi-110 002 (India)
Ph.: 23278000, 23261597

B.O.: No. 1015, Ist Main Road, BSK IIIrd Stage
IIIrd Phase, IIIrd Block,
Bangalore - 560 085 (India)
Visit us at: www.anmolpublications.com

Indian Women Writers in English

First Published, 2006

ISBN 81-261-2836-4

PRINTED IN INDIA

Printed at Mehra Offset Press, Delhi.

Contents

Preface

Right from my teaching career days I was interested in pursuing some creative work and my study of Nergis Dalal's fiction and her other journalistic writings and subsequent research on her, gave me a unique opportunity to fulfill my desire.

Indian writing in English, especially fiction, is gaining ground by leaps and bounds. Yet Indian English literary scene bristles with amazing anamolies and curious contradictions. Some writers like Mulkraj Anand, R.K. Narayan, Raja Rao and others have been given – excessive critical attention, while many others especially women writers have been neglected.

Nergis Dalal is one such writer, who can be said to have suffered unjust critical neglect. Even well-known scholars have not analysed her fiction properly. Though she has not been able to rise to the stature of Anita Desai or Kamala Markandaya, she is a versatile genius whose creative writing is not limited to the field of fiction alone.

The present study which is substaintially based on the findings of my doctoral research aims at thematic study of Nergis Dalal's entire work. The study includes not only her fiction but also her non-fictional writings.

I have discussed all her works in seven chapters in chronological order.

The introduction which forms the first chapter of the volume is a general introduction to the Indian English Novel and it also surveys the work of some important Indian women writers in English from 1950's onwards and makes an attempt to place Nergis Dalal in proper perspective among these writers.

Chapter two gives a brief sketch of Dalal's life, and discusses the influences that went into the making of her into a writer.

Chapter three is a critical study of Dalal's novel's *Minari, The Sisters, The Inner Door* and *The Girls from Overseas.* The themes that most stands out are -marriage, the problem of alienation and East-West encounter.

Chapter four is a detailed study of Dalal's collection of short stories, *The Nude.*

Chapter five is a study of Dalal's short story *The Birthday Present,* an excellent children's classic, which is very different from the rest of her short stories.

Chapter six studies critically Dalal's collection of middles *Never a Dull Moment* and *Other Journalistic Writings,* which focus on political and social life in India.

Chapter seven forms the conclusion, where the arguments of the preceding chapters are summarised and a cohesive picture is given.

I am happy to place on record that the author has been interviewed and is enclosed in an appendix.

Acknowledgement

It is with a great pleasure I record my sense of gratitude to my supervisor Dr.Ujwala P. Hiremath (Rtd.) Professor and Chairman, Department of Studies in English, Gulbarga University, Gulbarga for painstaking and guidance, which sustained me in the persuit of my study on Nergis Dalal's work with an unabated zeal.

No less is my gratitude to Prof. S.P. Hiremath, former Vice Chancellor, Kuvempu University, Shimoga who has been a source help and inspiration to me in all situations.

My sincere thanks are due to Prof. G.S.Balarama Gupta who kindled interest in me in the subject and guided at every stage in the preparation of dissertation.

I am really very grateful to my research author Nargis Dalal who has been kind enough to spare her precious time to discuss her works with me at her residence DEHRADUN, for her prompt answer to my questionnaire and for the critical material she has helped me with.

My sincere thanks are due to Dr. Mallikarjun Patil, Reader in English, Karnataka University Dharwad for his support and encouragement in completing my research work. I am also thankful to Dr.V.R.Badiger, Reader and Head Dept. of English, Gulbarga University, Gulbarga for his co-operation.

I am very much indebted to my father Sri. G.R.Javalgi to my wife Smt. Indumati and my children Amit, Abhijit and Anita from the inner most recesses of my heart for their sacrifice which has enabled me in attaining my present academic level.

Last but not least, I am very much thankful to Shri Kripal D. Joshi, Production Manager, Anmol Publications Pvt. Ltd., New Delhi for readily taking my work for publication.

—Dr. P.G. Javalgi

1

Introduction

The Indian Novel in English is an important branch of Indian English Literature, which had evolved historically as an effect of Britain's rule in India for nearly two centuries. Education being given to Indians in English, it was very natural for them to learn the art of novel writing in English as well, apart from writing in vernacular language to convey and propagate to their readers all over the country their patriotic feelings. India thus, produced a great number of novelists in the nineteenth century. As F.W. Bain said, "India, a withered trunk... suddenly shot out with foreign foliage". The use of English as a means of writing novels was so effective and convincing that it was welcomed from all corners of India.

The literary form of novel being new in the area of literature, it has gained great importance in India. Ever since it was introduced, it has created a great change and inspired many writers to contribute to its growth, and many more readers, to read and enjoy and learn from prose fiction. Earlier, they could engage in watching dramas and reading poetry, to enlighten and enliven themselves. When in the 19th century, owing to the Western influence, the novel as an art form took shape in India, it was liked and appreciated by all.

The Indo-English novel though a later arrival, thus established itself in the mainstream of modern Indian literature.

The function of literature being a true portrayal of life and society, the novel stands as the best means of the above.

Literary historians trace the beginning of the Indian novel in English to Bankim Chandra Chatterjee's *Raj Mohan's wife* published in the year 1864. He wrote two other novels in English *The Poison Tree* and *Krishnakanta's Will* which deal with social problems, a recurrent theme in Indian fiction. After Bankim Chandra Chatterjee, many others took to writing' novels in English. Among women, Rajalaxmi Devi was perhaps the first to write a novel in English. Her *The Hindu Wife* was published in 1874 and Toru Dutt's *Bianca* appeared in 1878. Ever since the Indian novel in English by women writers has made considerable and significant strides.

The Indian Novel in English by women may be divided into two phases. The first phase runs upto 1920 and the second phase begins in 1921. Women writers in English of the First Phase' were mostly autobiographical. Krupabai's *Kamala: A Story of a Hindu Wife* and *Saguna: A Story of Native Christian Life*, Shevantibai Nikambe's *Ratnabi: A Sketch of a Bombay High Caste Hindu Wife (1895) are* all autobiographical. However, Swarna Kumari Ghosal (1855-1932), Rabindranath Tagore's sister, wrote three romances: *The Fatal Garland* (1910), *An Unfinished Song* and *An Indian Love Story.* These women writers in spite of their inadequacies and limitations, have carved out significant place for themselves in the history of Indian English fiction. K.S. Ramamurthi credits the Indian woman writer of English fiction with a "Significant contribution to the growth of Indian fiction in the first phase of its history".

The Second Phase of the modern novel, which begins in 1920, the starting point of the Gandhian era, ends in 1947 at the dawn of Independence. This period saw the emergence, growth and development of the Big Three' of the Indian

Novel in English, viz., Raja Rao (1909), R.K. Narayan (1906-1999) and Mulk Raj Anand (1905).

The Big Trio'—R.K. Narayan, Raja Rao and Mulk Raj Anand—besides establishing Indian fiction in English as one of the authentic expressions of Indian life, have also inspired several young writers to take this literature seriously. They have, as a result, become the focal point of both national and international attention, and critical evaluations of their works are available in large numbers. Raja Rao sees people and society from his philosophical heights, whereas, Narayan's novels do not attempt a philosophical exposition of the Indian way of life. His involvement with Indian values and norms, however, is undeniable. Anand, on account of his ideological convictions, has boundless sympathy for the oppressed classes and equally boundless hatred for the exploiting classes. His fiction thus, deals with class norms more than the personal dilemmas of his characters. His *Untouchable* and *Coolie* discuss how the status of the neglected and the downtrodden could be raised and the rights of the people recognised.

Woman's writers of this period, unlike 'the Big Three', were unconcerned about the struggle for independence in their fiction, though thousands and thousands of women had participated in the freedom struggle. There is not a single novel by women to compare with Raja Rao's *Kanthapura* or even with Mulk Raj Anand's *Untouchable.* No woman writer writing in English has however, shown interest in national and social issues of the kind Anand deals with, though the arrival of Gandhi on the national scene in the 1920's turned into an emotional experience for most Indians, including women.

The women writers of this phase too were more or less autobiographical, living within a limited socio-psychological world. They were more concerned with problems in the domestic sphere, problems they had to face and deal with every day. Hence women writers have tended to limit their characters to achieving what they could within the confines of family life and daily routine of Indian society. No wonder, K.S. Ramamurthi accuses the Indian woman novelist of being "essentially a cynical creature given to more of dreaming and longing than to a serious preoccupation with the reality of the environment, for she had a marked predilection for turning inwards". The reason for this is not far to seek. The woman writer had to turn inwards in order to make herself understood by a world dominated by men for whom "a woman is either a repressed individual or merely a sex object. Woman as a thinking, sensitive human being"[4] has not been portrayed in their fiction long or short.

Indian women writers in English from the mid nineteen-fifties onwards –have been overtly expressive about women's problems and have dotted their fiction with women characters. The protagonists of almost all their novels and short stories are women. A brief survey of some established women writers in English will illustrate the point. Besides, we would be sailing considerably close to the subject of this thesis if we take note of the fact that Indian English women writers' are less written upon than their male counterparts. Whereas Anand, Narayan and Raja Rao have each elicited a dozen or so full length critical studies, there are not many women writers who have the distinction of having critical works written on them.

Ruth Prawer Jhabvala (1927-), like Kamala Markandaya, is an expatriate writer. Born of Jewish-Polish parents in Germany she married an Indian and came to India. She is an 'outsider-insider'; whereas Kamala Markandaya, born of Indian parents, married to an Englishman, and settled down in London is an 'insider-outsider'. "An important point of difference between Jhabvala and prominent western writers is that she has lived in India much longer with greater involvement". She has written eight novels and has published three short story collections. Her focus in all her novels—*To Whom She Will (1955), The Nature of Passion (1956), The Householder (I960). Get Ready for Battle (1962), A Backward Place (1965), Esmond in India (1968), A New Dominion (1973)* and *Heat and Dust (1975)*—is the intricate human relationships especially among women, in Hindu joint families. The other important themes she explores are marriage and the East-West encounter.

Jhabavala is perhaps the only woman writer who excels in presenting incongruities that have social, familial and cultural implications and she is probably the one woman writer writing in English whose fiction becomes a source of the comic too. She is indeed a substantial woman writer who earned the 1975 Booker Prize for her *Heat and Dust,* but is somehow excluded by some from the canon because of the multi-coloured content of her birth and area of operation. In the words of M.K. Naik "the most distinctive feature of Jhabavala's novels is the subtlety and adroitness with which she unravels the gossamer threads of intricate human relationships"[6]

Kamala Markandaya enjoys a significant place among Indian English writers. Most of her novels speak of her artistic talent and her extraordinary flair for writing. She has been a source of inspiration for several younger writers and also for research on her novels, which give wide scope for exploration. "She belongs to the generation of writers born and educated in the old order who could have been the pioneers of an off-shoot language with its own characteristic themes and idiom."[7]

Kamala Markandaya has nine novels to her credit—*Nectar in a Sieve (1954). Some Inner Fury (1955), Possession (1963), A*

Silence of Desire (1960), *A Handful of Rice* (1966), *The Coffer Dams* (1969), *The Nowhere Man* (1972), *Two Virgins* (1973) and *The Golden Honey Comb* (1977). In each of her novels except for the *Nowhere Man*, woman is the central character. Like Jhabvala, she too explores marital relationships. Like her again, the East-West encounter also finds a place among her important themes. In her work the East West encounter takes the form -first of a direct relationship between Indian and British characters and secondly of the impact of modern culture brought in by British rule on the traditional Indian life. Commenting on her writing, Robert Payne remarks: "She (Kamala Markandaya) knows exactly how to produce the effect she desires in a prose that is remarkably agile and completely her own. She could, I suspect, write about anything; she has an almost frightening skill".[8]

Kamala Markandaya proves herself to be one of the sanest women writers of the diaspora. In her own words,

> I do not think of myself as an expatriate writer. All my thought processes are Indian, my parentage, religion and schooling are Indian, all my formative factors are Indian.[9]

We may, however, mention that Kamala Markandaya's writing career has not always been smooth. Her *Two Virgins* created pungent controversy—not only among the general readers but also in academic circles when the academics of the University of Madras wanted this prescribed for study at the undergraduate level. In any case, the book did not receive enough positive comments. Markandaya is a writer of considerable vitality and significance and cannot be brushed aside merely because of the controversy that *Two Virgins* generated.

Naryantara Sahgal, a niece of Jawaharlal Nehru, the first Prime Minister of India, has written nine novels, two volumes of autobiography, and has contributed extensively to periodicals and is counted among the best political journalists of the country. She is considered by most critics, as a writer of political novels, but as M.K. Naik rightly says, "Politics is only one of her two major concerns... Her fiction is also occupied with the modern Indian woman's search for sexual freedom and self-realization".[10] From *A Time to be Happy* (1958) to *This Time of Morning* (1968) to *Storm in Chandigarh* (1969) to *The Day in Shadow* women and the marital problems faced by them occupy most of her attention.

Sahgal is a conscientious novelist with her own well-defined views on the art of fiction. Her interest in what she sees around herself and how she reacts to it has brought her to the sphere of fiction. Naturally, she, with her uncompromising rationalism, coupled with a consciously nurtured feminist dimension, has been inseparably associated with her family on the one hand and with her literary work on the other. In her own words, "I don't write for an audience. No writer does. I write for myself. In the process I hope I reach a wide audience".[11]

These lines throw light on her interest in a wide audience. Sahgal also confesses thus:

> I am Indian by blood, nationality, upbringing and conviction and western by virtue of my English medium education. My mother herself has the greatest satisfaction in abandoning what woman lib now calls the stereotype woman image and in setting out to succeed and sparkle in hitherto masculine field politics.[12]

This only shows that Sahgal has always endeavoured to live up to the values of freedom and a broad humanistic approach and its innumerable pains and pleasures.

Kamala Das, a bilingual Indian who writes both in English and Malayalam, is a force to reckon with. Often compared to Sylvia Plath because of the confessional nature of her poetry, she is also a skilled short story writer. Her *My Story* created a storm in literary circles: if it was treated by some as tricks to make money by writing veiled pornography, there were many others who offered exuberant kudos to her for her outspokenness in matters of sex and conjugal life. Kamala Das, in brief, is an unusually powerful writer with a burning social conscience, and to dismiss her as a writer of cheap pornographic stuff is to do injustice to a writer vibrant with the love of life in all its manifestations. In her works, "Several faces of Eve are exhibited... woman as sweetheart, flirt, wife, mother - - and above all, woman as an untiring seeker of the nature of the psychological processes behind both femininity and masculinity".

Anita Desai (1937 -), unlike Nayantara Sahgal, has nothing to do with politics. The emotional traumas faced by woman are her preoccupation. Her search for truth through the exploration of the psyche has resulted in a sensitive portrayal of several interesting characters. Her fiction seeks to unravel the complex responses of middle class women to their domestic world. In novel after novel she deals with what she calls the terror of facing single handed, the ferocious assaults of existence." Maya in *Cry, the Peacock,* Monisha in *Voices in the City,* Sita in *Where Shall We Go This Summer,* Nanda in *Fire on the Mountain* and Bimala in *Clear Light of Day* are women who are compelled to seek solutions to their problems through oppressive and exploitative norms of social and political acceptability. *Bye Bye Black Bird (1971),* is the only novel; in which social and political realities take precedence over probing of the mind."[14]

Not indistinctly reminiscent of Virginia Woolf and Dorothy Richardson, Anita Desai is a writer of such subtlety and sophistication that she has deservedly gained the reputation of being perhaps the most significant woman fictionist *writing* in English today. Her ability to use language symbolically,

women work out their own individual paths towards liberation and in the process discover new facets to their selves. In this discovery of their real selves and consequent self-fulfilment, these women pave the way for a better understanding of themselves as well as of others.

Like Nayantara Sahgal, Jai Nimbkar is—"A writer already known to the readers of magazines like *Imprint, Eve's Weekly* and *The Illustrated weekly of India* and is one of a growing number of authors," who has projected the predicament and agony of women in her fictional work. She hails from a family of eminent educationists.

Jai Nimbkar, the novelist, was profoundly influenced by writers like Somerset Maugham, Graham Greene, Margaret Drabble and Steinbeck. Like Maugham, she can be expedient, like Steinbeck she can write novels fraught with regional flavour. She drew inspiration from some of the Marathi writers like Vishram Bedekar, and Gangadhar Gadgil and Gouri Deshpande, who is her sister. Her characters ranging from illiterate farmers to socio-culturally conscious writers and intellectuals are all Maharashtrians drawn from the society around her.

Raji Narasimhan appeared as a critic with her book reviews and full length articles on various Indian authors. She has published five novels, two of them before the nineteen-eighties. M.K. Naik feels,

> Her third novel, *Drifting to a Dawn* (1983), is not as good as her second novel *Forever Free."*

Her *The Sky Changes* is steeped in an atmosphere of inexorable pain and melancholy. Atonement her fifth novel, also has unhappy filial relationships as its theme.

The women writers writing in English during the period from the 1920's through the 1970's have written about problems encountered by the middle-class woman. But a change seems to have come over the scene right from the 1970's.

Significant novels were also produced in the 1970's - some of them Sahitya Akademi prize winners, Chaman Nahal's *Azadi* and *The English Queens.* Arun Joshi's *The Apprentice,* Rama Mehta's *Inside the Haveli,* Anita Desai's *Bye Bye Blackbird* etc. - but the output was comparatively small. Usually the basic structure of literary history is found to be graphed in peaks and valleys, in the moments of fulfilment and barren periods. These periods are not sharply marked by specific dates and may well be coincidental and overlapping, and are composed of literary works, their authors, and the controlling temper and ideas of that time and place. Though there was no great spurt of creativity as in the 1960s or the 1980s, there was a steady literary output throughout this decade. Historically and politically, the 1970s were one of the most turbulent years in Indian history. The role of the 1970's in shaping the new Indian consciousness has been exceptional. The 1980s novel is the direct result of the events that occurred in the 1970's and the early 1980's.

Namita Gokhale, Shobha De and Arundhati Roy are some of the women novelists of the late 1980's and 1990s who concentrate on the problems of women but the problems they explore are very different from the concerns of either Jhabvala, Markandaya, Sahgal, Shashi Desphande, Anita Desai, Jai Nimbkar or even Bharathi Mukharjee. These novelists, specially Shobha De and Namita Gokhale, write about 'the new woman' whose moral, emotional and spiritual problems remain on the periphery.

Nergis Dalal, the writer chosen for this study is concerned with women's problems and social issues like most of the women writers noticed above. Her contribution warrants a full-length study. However, unlike most of the women writers writing in English mentioned above, she has been dealt with by literary historians rather perfunctorily and has received very little critical attention. However, even among women writers it is only a few like Anita Desai, Kamala Markandaya, Ruth Prawer Jhabvala, Shashi Deshpande and Kamala Das - that have received somewhat adequate critical attention. A host of writers talented but of a minor variety— have suffered from critical neglect, which they do not deserve. It is curious that very few critics have been persuaded to recognise the merits of writers like Mrinalini Sarabhai, Attia Husain and Vimala Raina.

Nergis Dalal's creative output is not very prolific. To date she has produced four novels, a collection of short stories and hundreds of middles and quite a few journalistic pieces. Her *Minari* was published in 1967 followed by *The Sisters* in 1973, *The Inner Door* in 1975, *The Girls from Overseas* in 1979 and a collection of the short stories entitled *Nude* in 1977. She is not a committed writer, a writer with a message. Perhaps because of this, her work has not drawn enough critical attention.

Though Nergis Dalal is a Parsi, "Her writings reflect no annuity of an ethnic nature because she in fact, has no strong ethnic identity".

In Nergis Dalal's novel Parsis are peripheral characters and the members of the Parsi family are almost caricatures. However, in *The Sisters,* the Parsi family occupies a central place. According to M.K. Naik, "it starts promisingly as a keen probe into jealousy but ends in melodrama". Her next two novels *The Inner Door* and *The Girls from Overseas* have no Parsi characters. Her writings do not reflect a sense of ethnic identity. And therefore to treat Dalal as a writer with ethnic identity would be an exercise in futility. Nergis Dalal herself says: "The concept of ethnic purity is a myth".

Thus Nergis Dalal is not a committed writer, but a writer of compulsion. 'A compulsion, as powerful and overriding as love or sex'. ... This study, therefore, rather than attempting to cull out a focused theme has concentrated on a study of her fiction without identifying any particular theme, because there is no sustained commitment to any one issue in her fiction. Even an admirer like O.P. Bhatnagar has to say this about the theme of East-West encounter in her novels. Discussion of the theme of East-West encounter in Mrs. Dalal raises the question whether her fictional world represents a westernized East or an Easternized West. Dr. Bhatnagar further observes thus: "There can be an Indian westernized way of looking at Indian life, which can be as native as the Indian way of looking at Indian life. The two modes are a reality in India today. And Nergis Dalal writes in both these modes with utmost ease. She does not strain to be Indian nor affect to be Western."

The intention of the present writer in, choosing Nergis Dalal for his research is not to establish her as a major Indian English woman writer. Neither the quantity nor the quality of her creative output warrants that. The contention, however, is that she does not deserve the kind of indifference and neglect that she has suffered at the hands of critics as well as historians. This is just a fervent plea for a fair-minded analysis and assessment of a writer endowed with enough talent to presage a fine promise or future.

The intention of the foregoing survey of women writers writing in English has been merely to indicate the brighter stars in the firmament of Indian English women writers-some not all, and have a broad idea of their achievement so that Nergis Dalal can be placed in a proper prospective.

REFERENCES

1. F.W. Bain, *An Incarnation of the Snow,* London, 1908, p. xv.
2. K.S. Ramamurthi, *The Rise of the Indian Novel in English.* New Delhi, Sterling, 1987, p. 66.
3. *Ibid.,* p. 42.
4. *Ibid.,* p. 42.
5. M.K. Naik, *A History of Indian-English Literature,* New Delhi Sahitya Akademi, 1982, p. 233.
6. *Ibid.,* p. 235.
7. Uma Parameswaran, *A Study of Representative Indo-English Novelists,* New Delhi: Vikas Publishing House, 1976, p. 56.
8. Rober Payne, *The Saturday Review.* 46, No 21, May 25, 1963, p. 34.
9. L.S.R. Krishna Sastry, *Essay* on *Indian English Literature in English* New Delhi: S. Chand and Co., 1991, p. 151.
10. M.N. Naik, *History of Indian English Literature,* New Delhi: Sahitya Akademi, 1982, p. 239.
11. *Indian and Foreign Review,* Vol. 10, No. 4. Dec 1, 1972, p. 19.
12. *Ibid.,* p. 18.
13. M.K. Naik, p. 209.
14. S.P. Swain, *Where Shall We Go This Summer?* in Manmohan K. Bhatnagar (Ed.) *Feminist English Literature,* New Delhi Atlantic Publishers, 1999, p. 247.
15. B.R. Rao, *The Novel's of Anita Desai: A Study,* New Delhi: Kalyani Publishers, 1993, p. 62.
16. Shobha Shinde, "Cross Cultural Crises," *The Commonwealth Review,* Vol. 4, 1992-93, p. 35.
17. *Ibid.,* p. 35.
18. Vanamala Vishanatha, 'A Woman's World, All the Way', in *The* (Ed.) *Fiction of Shashi Deshpande, ed.* R.S. Pathak, New Delhi; Creative Books, 1998, pp. 232.
19. P. Ramamurthi, "My Life is My Own," in Sushilan Singh, *'Feminism* and *Recent Fiction in English,* New Delhi: Prestige, 1991, p. 116.
20. Jacquelin Singh, 'A Taste of Bitter Rain', *Indian Review of Books,* Vol. 2, No. 8, May 16 – June 15, 1993, p. 30.

21. M.K. Naik, *Indian English Literature,* Delhi, Pencraft International, 2001, p. 88.
22. O.P. Bhatnagar, "Nergis Dalal", *Indian English Novelists,* in Madhusudhan Prasad (Ed.). New Delhi, Sterling, 1982, p. 133.
23. M.K. Naik, p. 243.
24. D.R. Sharma, The Art of Nergis *Dalal, "JIWE,* p. 18.
25. O.P. Bhatnagar, "Nergis Dalal", in Madhusudan Prasad (Ed.) *Indian-English Novelists,* ed., New Delhi: Sterling, 1982, p. 133.

2

The Making of a Writer

The decade of the 1950s is noted in the history of Indian English Literature for the emergence of a number of women novelists. According to Prof K.R. Srinivasa Iyengar,

> There has been a great tradition established by the women novelists, accounting for the success of women as novelists... Women are natural story tellers even when they do not write or publish.

One such woman novelist is Nergis Dalal who professes to write because she feels compelled to write "I am a writer by compulsion".

Nergis Dalal was born in 1920 in Panchagani of Maharhastra. It was a period of great ferment in the history of the national movement and it had its own impact on the consciousness of contemporary writers. There were some writers who favoured a non-violent and more or less peaceful expulsion of the British from India. In a way, their outlook could be characterised as Gandhian. In the second group, the writers advocated the expulsion of the British by any means peaceful or violent. It consisted of writers with—Marxist and terrorist sympathies. Perhaps these writers bore a deep impress on the family of Nergis Dalal.

The Indian novel in English between 1920 and 1950 derived its material largely from the national and political scene of

India. There are a large number of novels that deal directly with the national characters as the central theme and novels that use this experience as background to a personal narrative. The influence of the freedom movement was so widespread that the Indian novelists during the first four decades of the 20th century have written mostly about it. K.S. Venkataramani, Mulk Raj Anand, Raja Rao, Nayantara Sahgal, Kamala Markandaya, Manohar Malgonkar, to name only a few, have written novels on the freedom struggle. Besides dealing with the freedom struggle, they championed the cause of education of women and the uplift of the depressed classes. Dalal to a certain extent belongs to this category.

Nergis Dalal as a Parsi Zoroastrian was married to brigadier JAF Dalal in 1943 in Pune. In fact, her marriage with the brigadier influenced her writings to a certain extent. To quote her:

> My husband was in the Army and I used this as the background for some (certainly not all) of my novels.[2]

Unfortunately her husband died in a road accident in 1990. As a cartographer with the Survey of India, he became Surveyor General of India. Naturally Dalal travelled along with her husband all over India, saw the landscape and varied kinds; of social, political developments in the country. This provided her with capital material for her literary work. Dalal's literary interest developed as a compulsion to express her interesting thoughts and feelings. This only shows that Dalal has not become a writer overnight. She has developed some inner urge to give vent to her pent up feelings in her works.

It is important to note that Dalal's preoccupation with socio–literary activities was a result of the climate of the times in which she grew. The coming of independence at a price and the trauma of partition were responsible for the failure of the concept of brotherhood and the collapse of human values. This touched Dalal in the raw and served as the source material for quite a few of her novels. She was influenced by the new ripples of violence that erupted in the country in the 60s and 70s. In her own words,

> Being a woman writer, of course, has its own peculiar problems. Sometimes, I marvel that women ever manage to write at all. Not for us the bliss of finishing breakfast and locking ourselves into the study for hours of such uninterrupted work, while the house hums efficiently around us.[4]

Dalal's writings do not reflect her ethnic background. In fact, she has no strong ethnic identity. To quote her (speaking of herself in the third person):

> Two of her children married a non-Parsi, one a Tamil Brahmin, the other a Bengali. Like their parents, they too have no strong ethnic identities and they are comfortable with other communities and other ethnic groups.[5]

Dalal's writings usually lack in any well-defined ethnic identities. Roshan Dalal, her daughter rightly observes:

> She is a citizen of the world. Education, travel and mixing with others have ensured that she has no regional or ethnic identity. She has a quest for the eternal self, for something deeper in religion and thus identifies not only with Zoroastrianism but selectively with the religions of India.[6]

She is a writer with a specific urge to publish and one who would like to explore and define the areas of experience which have not previously been explored. She says that "a writer who has a genuine urge can easily publish his/her work. According to her, words can be seductive, and the constant pressure of inner mobility and psychological improvisation, parallel to the constantly shifting patterns of Society, needs finally to be subjected to the cool and critical eyes of a reading public". This only goes to show that as a writer, she wants to share her feelings and her deep felt convictions with others.

As a creative process, fiction writing is an expression of the most intimate awareness of the society in which it is born and in which it evolves. Small wonder, therefore, if the evolution of fiction and the evolution of consciousness of the societal mechanism and its dynamics are simultaneous and interlocked. By imaginatively treating the contemporary themes, Nergis Dalal seeks to explore and interpret life in its manifold aspects. According to her, fiction especially, of all forms of writing, is supposed to represent life and the fiction writer has to use as many aspects of life as are necessary to make his total picture convincing.[9] This only shows that Dalal has been inspired by the society around her and also by the urges and aspirations of the people. She has been able to portray powerfully, her own experiences, thoughts and feelings — her many frustrations, despairs, dreams, and desires.[10] So in a way, she essays an imaginative recreation of the society around her.

Nergis Dalal is an intellectual par excellence and her worldly knowledge is very profound. She loves to read, as well as write on the therapeutic value of books. She says: Indeed books are a barrier against despair; they shield against the hazards of everyday life; and they are an 'open sesame' into a magical world of the unknown where the normally tough if translucent membrane between the real and the imagined world is but a thin shifting veil. Despair, darkness, and depression are better faced with books, than with anything else. To be surrounded by books is, for a book lover, the ultimate delight.[11] These lines throw light on her interest in reading and also her thoughts that made her understand many readers.

Nergis Dalal is a conscientious novelist with her own definite views on the art of the novel. Her interest in what she seeks around and how she reacts to it has brought her to the sphere of the novel. She says: I have often been asked if I make an outline of my novels before writing. I think an outline is an excellent idea, but so far I have simply begun with an introduction, a theme or even a character and let it take me where it will.[12] These lines show that she may begin with a definite idea but it will take her in a different direction.

As a novelist, Nergis Dalal projects her own point of view and at the same time, she seeks to present men and things as she sees them. This is evident from what she says: I wrote novels in order to learn more about people and what makes them think. Also because I like to tell stories. Simone once said that we write and read novels because we all like to look through the keyhole and find out what others are doing or thinking.[13]

Hobbies like Yoga, diary writing, literary activities, gardening and environmental study are part of Dalal's life. Her experiences would certainly be reflected in her characters. In her own words, I write about the milieu to which I belong. Yoga has always been a passion of mine and therefore it makes its appearance.[14]

She even confesses that one should not write on matters which do not interest oneself. So she feels that an artist carries a certain responsibility, the inner self trying to understand the people around him or her.

Nergis Dalal is a person of discipline. She has travelled widely and thus she has gained much from the west. Like Nirad C. Chaudhuri and V.S. Naipaul, she too has her own strong views regarding the Indian way of life and style of functioning. She earnestly feels that people in India are not always well mannered, According to her:

> The editors pay scant attention to the writers who have no institutional connections or sinecure. The articles submitted to the press do not usually get acknowledged. Nor do the authors receive any word of appreciation.[15]

Dalal easily becomes critical of the Indian style of functioning. She earnestly feels that Indians are known for their demonstrations and bandhs. Once she saw some organisation in Uttar Pradesh agitating violently and obsessively for the sake of a separate state. She laments that a few political parties and people with their selfish motives disturb the whole pattern of life in the northern part of Uttar Pradesh. She does not appreciate any wayward agitations. Naturally, her characters are mostly disciplined individuals who would like to preserve discipline and order in society.

Though Dalal has travelled far and wide, she really does not appreciate undertaking continuous journeys. She observes: "Left to myself I have discovered that the best way of romance and the eternal beauty of strange places and countries, is through books. I have a pile of travel books and guides to such exotic and out-of-the-way places as Samarkand and Shanghai which are the source of never-ending delight. Sitting comfortably in warm, curtain-enclosed rooms, cross awesome rivers, sail down turbulent rivers and fight my way through dark impenetrable forests. Altogether enjoy to the utmost, the gold of the Savanna and the white silence out of my warm cocoon."[16]

As a writer, Dalal has written a lot about religion, yoga and meditation. According to her daughter, she writes on her own family and their oddities as well as idiosyncrasies or interesting aspects of the people she meets. She looked at each person as a human being, not a Parsi, Muslim or Hindu.[17] These lines show that she has observed the people around her closely, dispassionately.

Dalal feels that she must give vent to her deep felt convictions. In fact, her writing as well as stories characterise her life. She says: Writing is a compulsion, an escape from difficulties and hardships, a catharsis from the tragedy of life, a form of peace and spiritual freedom.[18]

Dalal's views on the use of language in a novel constitute an integral part of her theory of fiction. O.P. Bhatnagar rightly observes: "One sees in her novels the irrelevance of the supposition that it is only through an Indian language that an Indian consciousness can be expressed and that the attempt of the Indian novelist in English to depict the life of those whose emotional and intellectual life is fashioned by a different language is characterized by a total absence of the mutual nourishment between the writer and his society.[19] Dalal has made some observation even on her own use of language. She says, English is my native tongue, although my mother tongue is Gujarati. I was brought up in colonial times and like Nehru, I not only think in English, but dream in English as well'.[20] From this passage one can easily gather that Dalal is quite at home in the use of the English language to express her feelings and emotions. In other words, she writes with perfect ease, grace and flexibility thereby rendering credibility to her creations. As a novelist, Dalal has a few models before her. In her own words:

> One of my favourite authors is Graham Greene—a manic depressive who has survived into his eighties and who said writing, is a form of therapy in the human situation.[21]

Like Graham Greene, Dalal does not hesitate to create characters in order to display them in the conditions of torture.[32]

According to her a writer has the onerous responsibility of identifying himself/herself with the characters in their writings. One of her characters says:

> Do you think we are not sufficiently involved with life here? Perhaps we need to identify a little more with the people. After all, we are planning to spend the rest of our lives here.[23]

Even the novelist Dalal comments thus:

> The writer has finally a heightened responsiveness to the world. Even if he is looking at everything with an eye to putting it all down in black and white, he is really looking.[24]

Among Dalal's favourites the following women writers may be included. They are Nadme Gordimer, Candia, McWilliam, and Anita Brookner. Perhaps like these writers she too likes to put forth her feminist concerns. To conclude we may say that Dalal has set notions and objectives about writing. She has a clear perspective regarding her own themes and models. She writes of a protected world of the individual comprising subtle and complex emotions and passions, delicate memories, fragile fancies and evanescent moments, challenging values with powdered smiles and profuse ironies."[25]

We may tune in with Kamala Das in this context:

> I am an Indian, very brown, born in
> Malabar, I speak three languages, write in
> Two, dream in one. Don't write in English, they said,
> English is not your mother-tongue. Why not leave
> Me alone, critics, friends, visiting cousins
> Every one of you? Why not let me speak in
> Any language I like[7] The language I speak
> Becomes mine, its distortions, its queernesses
> All mine, mine alone. It is half English, half
> Indian, funny perhaps, but it is honest,
> It is as human as I am human, don't
> You see? It voices my joys, my longings, my
> Hopes, and it is useful to me as cawing
> Is to crows or roaring to the lions, it
> Is human speech, the speech of the mind that is
> Here and not there, a mind that sees and hears and
> Is aware."[26]

REFERENCES

1. K.R.S. Srinivasa Iyengar, *Indian Writing in English,* New Delhi, Sterling Publishing House, p. 435.
2. Letter from Dalal to the present writer dated 23-3-1999.
3. Nergis Dalal, 'On How I Became a Writer;' in R.K. Dhavan (Ed.), *Indian Women Novelists,* New Delhi: Prestige, 1995, p. 9.
4. *Ibid.,* p. 9.

5. Nergis Dalal in a letter to the present author dated 23-3-1999.
6. *Ibid.*, dated 23-3-1999.
7. Nergis Dalal, "On How I Became a Writer',' *Indian Women Novelists,* p. 10.
8. *Ibid.*, p. 10.
9. *Ibid.*, p. 10.
10. *Ibid.*, p. 10.
11. Nergis Dalal, "Living with Books," *Times of India, 12th* May, 1990.
12. *Ibid.*, p. 11.
13. Questionnaire, p. 162.
14. *Ibid.*, p. 162.
15. *Ibid.*, p. 162.
16. Dalal, "A Very Reluctant Traveller", *Times of India,* 3rd April, 1995.
17. Rosan Dalal, Ethnic Anxieties, the Parsis and Zorastnanism with reference to the writings of Dalal?" in Novy Kapadia and Ali Khan (Ed.), *The Parsis of Madyan,* New Delhi: Creative Books, 1998, p. 109.
18. Nergis Dalal, On How I Became a Writter,'p. 12.
19. O.P. Bhatnagar, "Nargis Dalal," *Indian English Novelists,* p. 131.
20. Questionnaire, p. 164.
21. "On How I Became a Writer", p. 13.
22. Boris Ford, *The Present.* London: Penguin Books, 1983, p. 84.
23. Nergis Dalal, *The Girls from Overseas,* p. 88.
24. On How I Became a Writer", p. 13.
25. O.P. Bhatnagar, p. 133.
26. Kamala Das, *An Introduction in The Golden Treasury of Indo - Anglian Poetry 1820-1965.* ed. V.K.Gokak, New Delhi: Sahitya Akademi, 1970, pp. 239-40.

3

Nergis Dalal's Novels

MINARI

The raw material of the novelist comes from the world in which he lives and breathes—the people he meets in real life – his family and relations, friends and acquaintances, beliefs and superstitions—all these leave an indelible mark on his heart and soul. When he creates his fictional world, they (the people in society) swarm into his memory and clamour for being reborn. Fiction transforms the actual world into an imaginary world. It is shaped by his imagination which embodies his vision of life and gives it a local habitation and a name. Nergis Dalal recreates the society round her in her novels in her own words:

> Fiction is supposed to represent life and the fiction writer has to use many aspects of life as are necessary to make his total picture convincing... The novelist lives, for the time he is engaged in writing, in a world that he or she creates imaginatively, which makes living in the real, objective world, something of a difficulty.[1]

In her four novels—*Minari, The Sisters, The Inner Door* and *The Girls from Overseas* – Nergis Dalal is actively engaged in recreating the society around her. She very ably projects an individual with "complex emotions and passions, delicate memories, fragile fancies and evanescent moments, challenging values with powdered smiles and perfumed ironies."[2]

Nergis Dalal's first novel *Minari*[3] deals with high class life at a hill station, with conventional characters (a Byronic hero, a vamp etc.) in stock situations. The novel celebrates with poetic facility, the scenic grandeur of *Minari,* a small hill station in Rajasthan, mauled by the former ruler Tejpore. The principal character is Anita, the daughter of a retired General, who is married to the faithful manager, Ranjan, of the Tejpore estate. Ranjan fials to provide romantic companionship to Anita. She is naturally drawn towards Tejpore, a charming personality. Soon, she realizes that Tejpore has led many women astray and that he is not the right person who can provide her with the right emotional fulfillment. Soon she returns to her husband's bedroom. Reconciliation takes place. Her husband's devotion is preferable to the exciting but amorous life-style of prince Tejpore.

Though prince Tejpore appears to have been pivotally positioned, the different characters resemble virisized and varicoloured bubbles which whirl around and touch one another, and break and disappear, and there is nothing substantial which stays in memory for long.

Tejpore is like a planet around which the rest of the characters in the novel orbit like satellites integration of his kingdom with the Indian union has proved a virtual blessing to him because now he is divested of the responsibility of ruling, though he continues to be the master of all the wealth of a princely state—to squander on races, motor rallies, and of course, girls. The magnitude of Tejpore's fabulous wealth is indicated in his description as a man who collected cars, women, and horses as other man collected stamps (p. 7). In addition, he is a man endowed with enormous personal charm and traits normal to a go-getter. Dalal is especially good at delineating Tejpore's personality:

> He was very handsome. Long and lean and dark, with the supple graceful walk of a well-fed panther, and the same exciting and dangerous qualities. His experienced face was a little lined, and the dark eyes, a little cynical and weary, but even these signs he carried off with an air, so that it was impossible to imagine him without them, impossible to feel that he would be improved by a lack of them (pp. 15-16).

Basically, Tejpore is a great lover. "He brought to the art of making love a sophistication, a subtlety, a finesse, all transmuted by experience into perfection (p.20). "He is match for Rula – nay, more than a match, if only we remember how they part at the novel. A widow in her thirties, Rula is bold and beautiful, talented and emancipated' (whatever that may mean), an upright woman with great zest for life, and conscious of all this. She was beautiful, successful and unattached. There were at least half-a-dozen men who would gladly have been more to her than just escorts" (p.21). That Rula's beauty is totally irresistible is evident from Dalal's repeated REFERENCES to it, and one of them runs thus:

> ... a woman in her middle thirties, with a magnolia skin gray-green eyes that tilted a little at the corners, and jet-black hair of an unusual silkiness that fell over her forehead like black feathers. There was, however, more to her than her beauty. She had the poise, the serenity, and the easy grace of an eighteenth century elegant. Of mixed Greek and Indian parentage, the perfection of her beauty was not always evident, giving place to tiredness or to signs of loneliness and neglect (p.13).

She is aware of Tej's blatant infidelities" (p.21) and would resist him if she could, but then, we know she didn't because she couldn't. Though at the very beginning of the novel she says that anything between Tej and her is a closed book, the book remains unshut till he parts from her. In spite of her being a combination of beauty, courage, and professional integrity, she is not above temptation when it comes to Tej. It is not unsafe, therefore, to assume that Rula is one of the territories that Tej conquers almost effortlessly.

Anita may be regarded as another territory which Tej conquers or nearly conquers, for it is possible to argue that it is not a conquest because Anita retreats before she could be conquered. According to the textual evidence available, it is Tej himself that she has to be thankful for. She owes her escape primarily to Tej's practice of not laying siege to a reluctant woman.

A huge chunk of the novels bulk is occupied by episodes relating to the General, Ranjan, Anita, Rula and Bim. The largest part of Dalal's attention is given to Anita and her tangential involvement with and last-minute escape from Tejpore and her subsequent engagement in painting. Anita is a housewife of conventional variety—blessed with a doting father, a husband who does not think of other women and two loving children.

Anita's placid life would not have suffered any disturbance if she had not come to be obsessed with the idea that her husband is too involved in his work to be able to spend not more than a couple of hours a day with her. She feels neglected and she broodingly magnifies it in her imagination. She nurses the idea so fondly, so recklessly, so continually, and so lingeringly, that she is easily taken in by the charm of Tejpore. Essentially naive and innocent and endowed with a knowledge of the world derived from books and not experience, she has all the potentiality to become one of Tejpore's victims. Anita becomes more and more miserable as she withdraws herself more and more from her husband whom intrinsically she loves dearly. When she learns that Rula and Tejpore have spent a night together she is so intensely fired by jealously that she walks up to Tejpore and flirts with him. When his face, so close to hers now that it is blurred, came down on hers, she turned and put her arms around his neck, returning his kisses with an ardour that startled him," (p. 98). However, Anita is basically a devoted wife. She cannot sustain her love for Tejpore for long, so she withdraws quickly from him. She realizes her folly and reflects:

> She had thought she was in love with Tejpore, and she could still see how exciting he might be, desirable and terrifying at the same time. But that was not what she wanted for always. For a little while perhaps, but not always. If she had to choose, then she wanted Ranjan—the safeness of his love, his obvious and unswerving devotion to her even though half the time he was preoccupied with his work. (p. 175).

Anita now finds solace and comfort in painting, thanks to the timely advice and encouragement offered by Mr. Wilten. And her ultimate withdrawal from Tejpore is seen in her act of giving away the painting that she has done of Tejpore.

It would be difficult to find fault with O.P. Bhatnagar when he calls Anita, "the emotional centre of the novel".[6] In fact Dalal bestows such loving and sustained attention on the Anita-Ranjan-Tejpore episode that one wonders if it does not act as a detriment to the structure of the novel. The focus is blurred; the reader's attention is disturbed, and the effect produced is diluted. It should not have been difficult for Dalal to develop the Anita episode into a separate and different novel and this concentration might have resulted in the production of a memorable novel, but, as it is, it looks rather like a square peg in a round hole.

The episode connected with colonel Rajendra Singh and Rula no doubt throws more light on the latter's character. She can shift her love from one man to another: she is so full of uncertainty and indecisiveness. "He (colonel, Rajendra Singh) followed her, standing just behind her, so that she was very conscious of his presence. She has no precise recollection of how she came to be in his arms, but the feeling was pleasant", (p. 112). But she does not approve of his proposal of marriage because he wants her to stop writing and that is something which she cannot do. Her faith in her own pen, in the efficacy of genuine Journalism; and her role as a journalist in shaping history - all these are firm and strong in her mind. And the reason she gives for not stopping writing is that it would 'diminish' her (p. 112), - a highly expressive word. All this is fine. But, then, it needs to be admitted that the episode throws more light on Rula than Tejpore, and, as a consequence, the focus gets somewhat deflected from the main story.

Sir Firoze and Lady Bharucha and their son Ferdie, the town gossip Mrs. Wheelers, Mrs. Evans & Zora, and a few others are interesting minor characters who touch Tejpore's life in some slight fashion or the other and they are characters who do not stick in the readers' memory, though each one of them has been drawn carefully, if somewhat sketchily.

Till we reach the climax, Tejpore has been drawn as an interesting rake, a charming breaker of hearts, a squanderer of wealth, an elegant lover who shifts from one woman to another with nonchalant ease and unabashed indifference to values, but it is only towards the end that the readers are given a knowledge of his dissatisfaction with the post-independence rulers of the country, his association with the ex-maharaja of Kunjara, his intimacy with Iqbal Singh and his anti-nationalistic attitude are revealed. All this sounds a bit contrived, theatrical, and unconvincing. The Tejpore - Iqbal Singh - Mehar Singh episode is no doubt interesting in itself and would perhaps have received a more careful treatment at the hands of similar writers better fitted to deal with such a theme as this, i.e., Mulk Raj Anand or Manohar Malgaonkar.

Dalal has very good powers of description as exhibited in respect of places described in the novel. For instance, look at the lovely description *of Minari:*

> Minari is a small hill station jutting out improbably from the

> plains of Rajasthan. Below it, the sandy wastes of the deserts stretch away into infinity, but here everything is cool and green and damp. Eucalyptus trees with their blue-green leaves and enamelled white trunks grow side by side with the date palms. The silver oaks were in flower, and everywhere the blaze of gold rippled against a monotone background of hills, shimmering and glowing for miles around. In the plains it was scorching hot, but here in the hills of Minari there was a silvery coolness. It was a twilight world, with the mist often enveloping everything in a pearly opaque light, so thick and dense that though surrounded by mountains, none were visible. And everywhere were the trees ripping, blurred, shadow-trees, formless and wet, flowing around the gaunt rocks like the sea, shadowy and insubstantial, like a badly developed photographic print (pp. 1-2).

By way of just one more example of this kind, we may cite the following,

> She passed *The Grange, The Retreat, The Wilderness* and *Bella Vista* and turned up towards the Crags. This was a walk she particularly liked. The road wound through craggy rocks, up and up to the top where a haze of blue faded away into the distance. Everything here was moist and cool. The cliff- fell away steeply into the valley four thousand feet below. Here too the mist drifted slowly over the hills, licking up little drifts of colour from the light so that the entire valley seemed to shine softly like a many faceted diamond. It was a world of improbable, mirage - like beauty. (pp. 9-20).

Two more instances - there are many more such in the novel no doubt- of Dalal's felicity of phrase—"the silver oaks flaming like some celestial conflagration" (p. 39) and "there was the sharp fizzy explosion of fireworks *scattering stars in the night*" (p. 43) (emphasis added).

Dalal's skill of description comes through as quite a match to her power of observation and that is revealed, for instance, in her brief but precise sketch of langurs:

> Langurs with their smoky gray fur, and black mask-like faces chattered in the trees, the mothers holding their small ugly babies with touching tenderness. Although they ate all her

> roses and geraniums, cramming the flowers into their mouths greedily, Rula could not help being amused by the creatures, distinguishable from humans only by the fact that they were incapable of laughter, (p. 71).

Though Dalal is not particularly known for humour, humour is scattered profusely through *Minari.*

Dalal can make her readers smile with just an appropriate word. For instance –

> Sons of sweepers and barbers," she was wont to say, turning up her *aristocratic* nose (p. 4.) (emphasis added).

Resorting to exaggeration is one of the usual ways humour is created and Dalal does it often as instanced in the following:

> He (Mr. Wilten) was capable of absently finishing at one sitting, a fruit cake which would have lasted an average sized family a week (p. 9).

Dalal may create a mild ripple of humour with a single phrase spiced with alliteration:

> I'm glad to see you are using fresh coffee and not that *detestable devil's brew* known as Instant coffee.[4] (p. 13).

Even Raja Mata finds it difficult to suppress a smile when Ferdie describes his father's yogic practice thus –

> Oh yes – he is as fit as a fiddle. He has taken up yoga now, and he spends the greater portion of his day standing on his head in the garden - it drives mother frantic. Whenever she wants to talk to him, he is either standing on his head-and it's not possible to talk to someone whose feet are where his head should be - or he is tied up in knots, like a boa constrictor. It really is quite extraordinary. (p. 38).

We also notice that Dalal is capable of creating comical characters like Sir Feroze and Zora. Here is Sir Feroze:

> Sir Feroze was standing on his head among the roses. He presented a very odd appearance, his thin elderly body, naked to the waist, his khaki shorts falling back over bony knees, his

> head reposing comfortably between bent arms. He rather liked the view that he obtained thus, upside down, with only the leaves and stems of the plants visible. He was mildly surprised to see Rula's feet move slowly into sight. He squinted at the watch on his wrist, sighed and lowered his feet. He stood up and greeted Rula affectionately. His face was pink, his eyes bright and shining. (pp 120-121).

And now we have Zora's amazing appetite:

> Meena brought in Zora's breakfast tray - and arranged it carefully on a small table across the bed. It was by any standards an enormous breakfast. Piles and piles of hot buttered toast, a large pot of coffee with cream, eggs, bacon, kidneys, and sausage were served in heated silver dishes, and a Jug of iced orange-Juice to finish off. Zora ate with concentration, gorging steadily, adding to those dazzling curves of generously displayed golden flesh. (p. 146).

The novel is replete with many more instances of Dalal's ability to use humour — in fact, so many of them that one wonders why she has not cared to use this tool with greater profusion and force and earned herself a claim to be rated as a top-ranking humorist.

Dalal is quite capable of sarcasm — quiet and therefore deadly. The following extract should serve as a typical illustration.

> MINARI, DROWSING THROUGHOUT THE YEAR, COMES BRIEFLY to life in the summer. Long brilliant cars jam the narrow roads, as the plains disgorge their dispirited load of humanity on the hills. It is always astonishing to see how many Government departments find it absolutely essential and necessary to their work to hold conferences in Minari instead of in Delhi (p. 158).

Occasionally Dalal may be faulted on using a stale simile, which is indicative of sheer laziness. For instance, here is a reference to Sir Feroze—"Oh yes - he is as fit as a fiddle". (p. 38) and another to the colonel – "The Colonel stepped in smiling and composed and neat as a new pin". But we have plenty of instances to prove that she can create similes, which are both fresh and innovative. For example—

> "*The lake was rippled by a breeze and green as a cat's eyes,* the boats rocking gently at their moorings." (p. 59) (emphasis added).
>
> and
>
> Although it was hot and sunny outside, the atmosphere inside Rula's house was cool, *like a chilled drink.*" (p. 71) (emphasis added).

One is reminded of Mohun Biswas in V.S. Naipaul's *A House for Mr. Biswas* where Biswas struggles to arrive at authentic selfhood. Similarly Anita in *Minari* persistently gropes for meaning in life and a sense of selfhood. Mohun Biswas's problems are mostly economic but Anita's problems are emotional and psychological. Biswas is a wanderer with no place he could call his own, with no family except that which he was to attempt to create out of the engulfing world of the Tulsis. For with his mother's parents dead, his father dead, his brothers on the estate at Felicity, Dehuti as a servant in Tara's house, and himself rapidly growing away from Bipti who, broken, became increasingly useless and impenetrable, it seemed to him that he was really quite alone.'[8]

Biswas, frustrated by a series of unsuccessful jobs, ultimately becomes painter. It is on one of the occasions of sign painting that he enters the Tulsi House. He realizes the security and solidity of the house and the support its members can offer at the time of crisis. He is quite confident of the economic and emotional security he would receive from the House.

Mr. Biswas needs this sanctuary. It is his refuge from his own failures and anxieties. It also satisfies his self-serving human need to be part of a powerful, wealthy and respected family, it is a bulwork against his feeling of nothingness, however much he may subconsciously resent this, and its very solidity - something he has never known before - provides him with warmth and sustenance and assurance."[9]

Thus the growth of Biswas to selfhood is linked with his shifts from one house to another until he finds a house of his own. The true house becomes an integrating metaphor in Biswass expanding and diffused consciousness.'[10]

Dalal's Anita's conflict is psychological, impelled by the desire to demonstrate her human necessity. Wilton discovers her skill as a painter. He urges her to take to painting "as it would give you something to do". (p. 196) He provides her with books to read about painting techniques. Fascinated by the books and her own latent talent, Anita finds selfhood and contentment in the expression of a creative urge.

The very act of painting absorbed all her attention. (196) Absorbed in painting she no longer remains idle. Anita converts a small dressing room into a studio and spends most of her day there. Her paintings had a childlike freshness of vision and unselfconsciousness. Trying to improve her performance became Anita's preoccupation in life. Mr. Wilton is delighted that Anita's talent as a painter has not only given a new meaning to her life but saved her marriage as well: She was glad to see Ranjan but now if he were silent, preoccupied, she did not in the least object. She too had her own thoughts—she too seemed just a little absent-minded". (p. 197).

Mr. Wilton with a feeling of self-congratulation noted that Anita's obsession with painting helped to hold together a marriage that was becoming a little shaky at the roots". (p.197) Nergis Dalal's novel is an authentic sociological study of the quest of selfhood on the part of Rula and Anita in a very upper-middleclass milieu. There are no idealistic solutions. Anita's skill as a painter is not a fairytale road to success. Towards the end of the novel, when Rula goes to say goodbye she discovers Anita absorbed in painting. Observing her work, Rula realizes: There was nothing wrong with the painting, except that it had no authority. It was the work of a good amateur." (p. 232) Anita is still cheerful. She realizes her limitations. As she tells Rula, she needs years of experience. So though no genius, Anita is a talented painter engrossed in trying to improve her technique. Above all, painting helps her exorcise the memory of Prince Tejpore. She paints an exaggerated portrait of Prince Tejpore from memory. She tells Rula that the exaggeration is deliberate and is "a sort of catharsis for me. I felt much better when had finished". (p. 234). She presents the picture to Rula who willingly accepts it.

So painting helps Anita find a meaning in life. Her quest for perfection will take years. However she is willing to persevere with no guarantee of success. It gives her emotional satisfaction and a new perspective to marriage, Ranjan's late hours, and emotions for Tejpore. Her choice is individualistic, a quest for selfhood through painting.

The foregoing analysis is presumably sufficient to infer that *Minari,* no doubt, has most of the ingredients to make a good novel but here the result in reality is a pot-pourri which provides the reader with an adequate glimpse of Dalal's potentiality and promise rather than any memorable fulfillment. The safest, and probably the sanest, verdict on the novel was passed by D.R. Sharma, one of Dalal's early critics: "... espite a pot-pourri (sic) feudalism and modernity, of sex and brandy, of journalism and morality, of hauteur and compassion, *Minari – remains* an interesting weak novel"

THE SISTERS

While *Minari* deals with Anita's search for meaning. Nergis Dalal's novel *The Sisters*[11] concerns itself with a contrastive study of twins at opposite poles both physically and mentally,'" It deals with the pathetic life of Rita, who has to suffer neglect and humiliation both at home and outside, because of her not being born as beautiful as her twin sister Nina".[13]

Spun around the principle of near-mathematic precision of antithesis, Dalal's second novel, *The Sisters* relates the story of the childhood, youth and tragic end of Nina and Rita, the non-identical twins of a Parsi household, locked in eternal jealousy, constant heart-burn, and ruthless intriguing and the resultant disaster and destruction.

The contrast between the twins is highlighted and heightened right from the start. Nina is born lovely - with a creamy skin, silky hair, and eyes "so dark a green that they were almost black" (p. 5). So much so that she is effortlessly graceful and beautiful"(p. 5). Rita, on the contrary, with her dark skin and rough curly hair, is lumpish and plain' (p. 6), an ugly duckling, in essence.

Naturally, therefore, the world treats Nina with respect and admiration and Rita with disgust and derision.

The psychological distancing between the twins is accentuated by the tactless way they are treated by their own mother, Sophie. We find a clear instance of this on the sixth birthday of the children, both dressed in lovely and expensive garments imported from Harrods. Whereas Sophie is exuberant in greeting Nina, "Oh darling, you look beautiful !"(p. 10), she accosts Rita with. "Honestly, if you don't look pretty in this, I don't see how you ever can"(p. 10).

It is not that Nina is positively endowed in every respect and Rita is devoid of praise worthy qualities in toto. Rita is extraordinarily intelligent and wins scholastic accolade all along.

Another blessing which Rita has and Nina is without the affection of the grandmother.

In fact, it is this grandma that proves to be Rita's saviour and guardian angel. She advises the girl burning with jealousy and simmering with hatred thus:

> Nina is pretty and you are not. That's the way it is and that's the way it's going to be. You can't go through life tearing up things to prove that you are as good as she is. You have to learn to do all the things Nina can't do. You are clever, she isn't. See that you do well in school. Come first in everything, win all the prizes. Make yourself known as a brain. Don't compete with Nina - be different. (p. 20-21).

That is heartening enough to the depressed child. In a bid to get confirmation of the grandma's, affection, she says, 'But you love me best, better than Nina'(p. 21). The answer is a positive 'Yes, I love you best' (p. 21).

That is a turning point in the life of Rita, and inescapably in that of Nina too:

The sisters grow up - Nina as an ethereal beauty and Rita like an overstuffed laundry bag.

And they branch off differently too.

Nina is married off to a handsome young man, Bobby Mehta, a millionaire's son. The dazzle and the glitter are, however, short lived. Bobby is discovered to be impotent, there's a slump in business, and Bobby himself dies eventually in a car accident. That leaves Nina crestfallen and bewildered, but soon, she recovers and starts living a free and promiscuous life.

Rita, on the other hand, flowers into a studious intellectual, does her graduation and post-graduation creditably, and even starts doing research for a doctorate. Meanwhile she inherits her grandma's entire wealth not excluding jewellry. Now she comes in contact with Ramesh, an architect and his family. She agrees to help Ramesh's parents with a fabulous sum for the dowry of Sunita, his retarded sister, and marries Ramesh. Rita's attitude to marriage is pragmatic. There is no place for romance in it. She says: "I had in a sense, bought Ramesh and he was grateful." The marriage, initially, is successful enough. Ramesh forges ahead in his career as an architect with no time or inclination for romantic overtures or flirtations.

If only Nina and Rita had moved in their respective orbits, they could have avoided tragedy for both but fate seems to have willed otherwise.

Nina's visit to Rita, though apparently casual, proves fatal. Strange as the alchemy of sexual attraction is, Ramesh, hitherto impervious to feminine charms, falls a quick prey to the machinations of Nina, by now an adept at seduction. Love, especially of the clandestine variety, can scarcely be hid and Nina's affair with Ramesh does not go unnoticed by Rita.

This is very clear in her letter to Ramesh, which unfortunately reaches Rita:

> My dearest darling,
>
> Your letter made me wildly happy. At last, after all these months, we will be together always, I can't tell you how I have lived all this time, for only this moment, with only this hope. It does not matter at all to me whether R. divorces you or not, but if it affects your career then, of course, we must be properly married. You say you do not anticipate any trouble and that Rita has never been either possessive or emotional. But you don't know her as I do. She is capable of violence and viciousness. I can't see her letting you go without a struggle, even though you are now making enough money not to be dependent on her. But together we will cope with anything.

> You say you plan to tell her soon. I will be praying for us both.
>
> *Your very own*
> *Nina*

She settles a thousand rupees per month on Nina and wants her to quit post-haste. In the meantime Ramesh too proves ungrateful. With no qualms of conscience, he wants his legally wedded wife Rita to agree to a divorce, which will leave him free to legitimize his unabashed indecency illicit relationship. "I want you to divorce me, I want to marry Nina" (p. 144). This brings another shock and blow to Rita. As a result, Rita is startled but plots and plans her strategy coolly and consummately. And, with the help of her family doctor, Narendra, she drugs Ramesh and sees him dead with quiet and determination. As M.K. Naik puts it "This novel starts promising as a keen probe into jealously but ends in melodrama".

This, in brief, is the story of *The Sisters*.[8]

The theme of jealousy is, no doubt, a powerful subject for a literary work. However, if Shakespeare could make a high voltage tragedy out of it in his *Othello*, Dalal's novel is patently weak in its amplitude and impact. Though it is perhaps unfair to institute a comparison, of this kind, we can't help admitting that the impression that the novel leaves on the reader's mind is neither profound nor lasting. Maybe what it basically lacks is an adequate objective correlative.

Like a well-made play *The Sisters* so neatly and accurately designed on the principle of contrasts that it fails to escape the charge of being disappointing.

Nina is physically pretty and attractive whereas Rita is plump and plain but brainy.

The whole world loves Nina, for she has beauty but the

grandma loves Rita and bequeathes all her fabulous property to her and not to Nina, no, not even to her own son.

Nina marries the handsome son of a rich man but he proves to be a good-for-nothing impotent and the riches evaporate, whereas Rita has money, two wonderful sons, a beautiful house, and a husband progressively rising in his career.

And, sometime later, that is when fortune has let down Nina and looked kindly upon Rita, it is a neat tug of war between them.

Driven by despair, Nina visits Rita and there she plans to entice Ramesh, and, in fact, succeeds in seducing him and even wants to marry him. When Ramesh asks Rita for divorce, the latter does not yield initially. But when she does, it is only to plot his death.

When the world around Nina has totally crumbled, Rita may appear triumphant but she too has been deprived of Ramesh and hence forfeited her peace of mind.

The story-line, thus developed, by Dalal is too inadequate to express the theme powerfully and memorably.

Excepting Nina and Rita, the other characters in the novel are not well developed. They are either anemic or unnatural and that contributes not a little to the failure of the novel.

The grandma choosing to bequeathe her property not to her son but one of the grand daughters sounds rather unnatural. The son himself is both anaemic unnatural, because he rarely exercises any influence on either his wife or his daughters. And Sophie is no different from her husband. She keeps praising Nina decrying Rita, though they both happen to be her children. Instead of being a "flesh and blood", human being, she looks like a mere marionette.

The Sunita episode does not seem to integrate well with the main story of novel.

One is struck by the inanity of such snatches of dialogue between the twins as the following:

> I should have thought that all your lovers would have given you enough Jewellery and even perhaps houses, to last you a life time? (Rita) (p. 131).
>
> I slept only with those men with whom I was genuinely in love. I suppose that sounds very strange to you, so cold, so calculating. You wouldn't understand what it is like to be romantically in love with a man. (Nina) (p. 131).

Or, look at this bit of conversation between Rita and her prospective mother-in-law:

> If we hope to marry her (Sunita) off well there has to be a good dowry and this we can only get if we ourselves demand a good dowry for Ramesh. You understand?" (Ramesh's mother).
> I understand ...How much will be enough?"
> Fifty thousand. Is that too much ?
> No, no. Fifty thousand and later perhaps a small house for her."
> Her eyes shone. You are not pretty, but you are good." (p\. 44)

Dalal seems to be fond of making now and then, generalizations which are ramming in the fact of Rita being a 'plain Jane' once too often, so as to cause distaste in the reader for the novelist's method of laying it on too thick. Too sweeping to be unassailably credible.

Let's go through the following extract from *The Sisters,* a rather long disquisition on romantic love:

> THE IDEA OF LOVE—romantic love that is—was conceived and born in the European mind. An oriental, an Indian, does not necessarily expect marriage and love to go together. Centuries of breeding from marriages that were cynically or

> pragmatically arranged, had given Ramesh a purely rational expectation. Marriages were from convenience, (how else get the regular sex so necessary for health?) to cement or repair fortunes, to beget children. There were no starry-eyed illusions about sharing everything, loving each other for ever, or belonging one to the other in a surrender so complete that nothing was held back, nothing restrained. He did not expect any of this and in a sense that made my task easier. For most men, (and this is probably true of other countries as well) their careers, their work are infinitely more important than the women they marry or sleep with. Wives, children, mistresses - these are secondary to the High glitter of a successful career (p. 47).

At best what Dalal says maybe a half-truth, and half-truths can be more dangerous than falsities.

Now, look at this short statement by Sukhbir.

> The whole point of all this shooting and killing is to show how male you are ¾ a sort of substitute sex symbol. In fact I have a theory ¾ the man who shoots and kills with the greatest enthusiasm is the one who is compensating for his lack of sex (p. 66).

Or this from Sukhbir again:

> The beautiful ones, he said, "they are handicapped from the beginning. I will write a book about it one day. Their beauty makes them neglect everything else - brain, heart, feelings. They are crippled emotionally - dangerous in their self-involvement. When they sleep with a man, they see only themselves in his eyes. Always, they are watching themselves. No relationship with them can be anything but a failure. If I had a son, I would tell him, never, never marry a beautiful woman (p. 69).

This sort of theorization, whether an authorial projection through a mouthpiece serving character, or the characters own, has as much chance of being false as true.

One more example from the text

> I SAID TO Nina, I have never understood why you did not return to Hyderabad to live with Sophie. You were always her favourite and it would have seemed the sensible thing to do.
>
> "For a long while Nina was silent and then she looked up and shrugged.
>
> Sophie adored me as a child. When I grew up, we had nothing in common. I went home when father died and found a stranger. Someone with whom I had no point of contact and who even repelled me. Besides, can you see me living quietly all my life in a house with another women, even if that women did happen to be my mother? I would have died of boredom (p. 75).

Resenting the mother as just another woman sounds somewhat unnatural!

The intention of furnishing all these short and long quotations is to suggest that cumulatively they contribute to the overall failure of the novel to become a memorable work of art.

It is not that Dalal is incapable of producing beautiful descriptions. Take for instance, this sketch of Rita's house and its surroundings:

> Bars of bright wintry sunshine fill the rooms, glinting on the polished floor lavishly covered in Turksih and Bokhara rugs. From Nina's room upstairs I look out on the rose garden and the curved gravelled drive that sweeps with cushions of Siamese pink. The lawns today are gilded by the sun and the fountain sends up a silvery rainbow of water. Marching at the back are the trees—the peach and plum with ruffles of pink and white blossom, and the teak, plum and oaks, shedding red and orange leaves and glowing as though made from bronze leaves and glowing as though made from bronze. Circling the whole house are the hills – deep purple pale blue, or colourless as still water. On misty days they disappear altogether and there is nothing then but the sky, touching the tops of the trees. It is a beautiful house – my house (p. 6).

One of the finest passages in—the novel, reproduced hereunder, clearly indicates Dalal's descriptive abilities.

> Behind us, more people had collected and then it began, with the beating of drums and blowing of conches, as the lamps on the brass trays blossomed into yellow flowers, a semi—circle of quivering light scattering and reforming into formalized patterns, sometimes blurred, sometimes sharply etched on the lambent night, floating over and sinking into the water, till there seemed a chain of yellow flowers forming inside the darkened depths, and all the while the drumming and the clanging continued and around us rose the repeated soft cries of *Ganga Matc ki jai* (p. 110).

She can write not only aptly but strikingly, too; for instance, she can use an expressive simile:

> I let my eyes roam idly over the shabby room — the two shabby armchairs whose stuffing seemed to be leaking out slowly like the dying breath of an old man (p. 44).

She can also write sentences in which every word tells;

> Ramesh's father was a stooped old man, wearing a loose shirt hanging out over pyjamas, and a lined defeated face. His was one of those lives in which nothing ever seems to come out right (p. 45).

Or, she can write aptly and at the same time amusingly. For example we have her brief but telling sketch of Sophie put into the American smuggler's mouth:

> A remarkable woman, your mother. Marvellous business sense and what she doesn't know about this business you could stick on a ten-cent stamp. I do believe she is one of the most important dealers in this line, in any country (p. 83).

Some of the episodes in the novel like suphie's business with her smuggler clients and the trip to Hardwar are both good and amusing.

But, fiction is not all about description and fine writing. It is characters in the round and the density of life portrayed that provide 'ballast' to a novel.

One tends to agree with D.R. Sharma when he says that "as a work of art it (*The Sisters*) stays on low slopes". And the probable reasons are to be located in Dalal's inability to sustain her creative energy to match her mighty theme. The trouble with this novel is that it falls between two stools it is neither a good short story nor a good full-fledged novel. The novel on the whole is disappointing, as Jai Nimbkar, a fellow women writer has put it, though O.P. Bhatnagar is all praise for the technique of the novel.

Written from a feminine perspective, the novel explores the attitude to marriage and human relationships, through the changing perspective of Rita. She is the ugly twin with an unhappy childhood, later a successful student and rich housewife. The events do not move in a linear progression. Instead the author uses a flashback technique, like that of Kamala Markandaya in *Nectar In a Sieve,* though, unlike as in *Nectar in a Sieve,* the flashback does not move in linear fashion O.P. Bhatnagar rightly observes:

> The technique of flashback and memories has been so intricately woven with the narrative in the present that it brings the whole drama of a hurt feeling and irony with an intensity and compactness rare in the whole range of Indo-English fiction.[14]

The novel starts in the present. Rita is fifty years old, a widow, loaded with money, with two children, beautiful houses in Dehra Dun and Mussoorie and security. Her twin sister Nina, is coming to stay with her. Nina is the archetypal child of beauty, with *pale* creamy skin and masses of silky hair and eyes of a dark green shade. (p. 5). She is expected to be the successful and happy twin. Yet her life is insecure. Her husband Bobby had died in a car accident at Belgrade having squandered all his money in business transactions. Nina's financial affairs are insecure.

Awaiting her sister, Rita reflects on their childhood. Using the flashback technique, the past is unfurled. Sitting together and talking, the twins recall their good old days. Questions and promptings by Nina lead Rita to recall the past. Unlike Kamala Markandaya's *Nectar in a Sieve,* the flashback does not move in a linear progression as already pointed out. Gasps of reality are conveyed through the perceptions of Rita, invariably reacting to a memory or a conversational opening provided by her glamorous twin sister Nina.

The reality of Rita's childhood is unhappiness. Even thinking about it makes her stomach muscles tighten and shrink. 'Their family lived in Hyderabad, in pre-independence India. The father Feroze was employed by the Nizam in the Mint. The twins stayed in a sprawling mansion with their parents and rich maternal grandmother. Rita with rough curly hair, dark skin and plump figure was always contrasted unfavorably with her slim, fair and attractive sister Nina. As they grew up, Nina, effortlessly graceful and beautiful, was the centre of attraction, at their birthday party, social gatherings, school pantomime and dance parties. The English mother Sophie always doted on Nina. The fundamental colour consciousness of most Indians made people, from a photographer to admiring young men adore Nina and neglect Rita.

THE INNER DOOR

While *The Sisters* concerns itself with Rita's search for meaning, Nergis Dalal's third novel *The Inner Door* seems a natural sequel to *The Sisters*[6] because it deals with Rahul who assumes several roles in his quest for selfhood. Rahul, a delicate and handsome young boy, comes of a poor family. The sudden death of his father takes him to his uncle in Rishikesh where he runs a yogik Ashram. On the way he is spotted by the Americans Chris and Myra — who plan to use him commercially in yogik trade and offer to pay a substantial amount. In return after a series of experiences he renounces everything and goes for further spiritual attainments into the mountains.

Writers—Anglo-Indian as well as Indo-Anglian are found to have been interested in presenting India as a country replete with curiosities and contrarieties like beggars and princes, jungles and tigers, flood and famine. And yogis and sanyasis.

Yoga is a discipline, which has physical as well as spiritual dimensions. It is pursued by charlatans as well *as* authentic seekers - of course for diverse reasons. Dalal has a extensive, as also an intimate knowledge of all these aspects of yoga and yogis as they are prevalent in India and abroad alike. She is aware of the possibility of the co-existence of such opposites as fake fakirs and genuine *Sadhakas,* spurious *sanyasis* and genuine seekers after truth, and hypocrites and authentic souls. Further, Dalal is aware that a sinner may become a saint or he may continue to parade himself as a saint even while remaining a sinner in essence.

Dalal puts all this knowledge of yoga of the true and spurious variety to use and projects it fictionally in her third novel, *The Inner Door.* The central theme of this novel, broadly speaking, is the perennial contrariety of appearance and reality. Putting it in other words, we may say that the theme is the transformation of an apparently ordinary man into an extraordinarily self-realized soul. It is the saga of a young man who masquerades for some time as a yogi but is eventually impelled to throw away the mask and set out in quest of the real and eternal. The protagonist, though a spurious Swami to start with, ends up as a genuine *guru.*

A close look at all the ashrams with which Rahul comes in contact would help us not only to trace his spiritual evolution but also give us a glimpse of different varieties of dealers in yoga and spiritual aspirants - of the spurious variety and the genuine kind alike.

The first spiritual leader that Rahul establishes contact with is his own uncle, Swami Jagadish, who has become a sanyasi not because of any overwhelming spiritual compulsion, but only in order to vanquish his belligerent wife. Dalal's narration of this story is refreshingly crisp and scintillatingly witty and merits quotation despite its length:

> In his orange robes, his head shaved, the tilak mark on his forehead, he might appear to her (his sister) almost unrecognizable He had never regretted taking Sanyas-diksha. He only wondered that he had waited so long. Married to a woman who alternately nagged, whined and screamed, he had taken refuge for years in a silence so thick and impenetrable that it had increased her frustration and fury to hysterical heights. She had given him, through the years, one whining daughter, for whom he felt not the slightest affection.
>
> In the old days, one of his silent fantasies was to imagine ways of killing his wife. It was a process that was guaranteed to divert his mind from her stupidity, and provided him with many hours of happy musing.
>
> There were, it seemed, an infinite variety of ways in which one could murder a person, but not alas! dispose of the body. Watching her sleeping, her face heavy and wrinkled with lines, bad temper and spite etched deeply into the flesh, he would imagine picking up a pillow from his bed and holding it firmly over the sleeping face. How good it would be never to hear that voice again. Unfortunately; the police were so clever these days, they were sure to find out how it was done. Perhaps he could poison her with some unknown poison, or inject her with air, like die Nazis had done to their victims, or push her down the stairs so that she broke her neck. He had been an avid reader of murder stones and each one provided him with a fresh idea. In reality, of course, he never had the slightest intention of killing her and imperiling his immortal soul, but he found the imaginative process extremely enjoyable and often became so engrossed in these inner processes that he smiled and laughed to himself, sending her into frenzied fits of rage.

> At last, when he could no longer stand the sight of her face, the sound of her voice, when killing her had become a tempting reality, he simply walked out, took a bus to Rishikesh and attached himself as a disciple to the first ashram. He had been a good chela and when his Guru died he took over from him. There was nothing his wife could do about it, although she was made manic with frustration. He was merely following the good and respected Indian tradition of the householder giving up everything to devote himself to a search for God. She could not even sue him for support because he had taken nothing. Society did not took upon her as one in need of either sympathy or support, and in his own way, he had been happy. He sometimes regretted the fact that the ashram was so small and attracted only those with little money. Across the river, high into the hills was the Maharishi's palatial building, glittering with lights and opulent with marble floors and quantities of silver. He had once considered himself a disappointed romantic. Now he was resigned, ready to make the most of whatever each day brought to him. He ate well, was respected, could live his own life without interference, and looked forward to each new day with unfailing optimism (pp. 12-14).

To emphasise the point that Swami Jagadish's ashram is probably the poorest in Rishikesh and also to indicate that its owner is still somewhere at the bottom of the spiritual ladder, Dalal gives a graphic description of the inside of the ashram thus:

> The courtyard was damp and had a smell of rats. A long narrow corridor divided the ashram into two—on one side small residential rooms and on the other the kitchen, the prayer-hall, the washing places. The prayer hall was decorated with garish pictures of dark blue Krishna playing flutes, garlanded with tinsel and thread. There were other gods of the Hindu pantheon decorating the walls and at the furthest corner in massive letters was the sacred OM.
>
> Their room was cabin-like, with two string - beds, a table, a chair. Rahul was expected to share a room with his mother and for the first time he felt her constant presence, oppressive. They were called for lunch almost immediately and Rahul was pleasantly surprised at the excellence of the food. His uncle might lead a Spartan existence but the asceticism evidently

> did not extend to food. There were *thalis* of deliciously cooked vegetables, rice, dal, poories, good pure ghee and curds. There were freshly made hot and delectably soft laddus (pp.14-15).

The purpose of these long extracts is to indicate the quality of spiritual life that is enshrined in this ashram. It is all earth - earthy and commercial through and through.

The second and third instances of charlatanism are given to us through Chris's experiences in the States. The second one relates to an encounter with an Indian Swami who pretends to be endowed with magical powers, and dupes the Americans of a thousand dollars by asking them to close and open their eyes. In Dalal's words:

> The first time he had paid his dollar and entered a gloomy looking hall in which roughly a thousand people sat, waiting. A spotlight flickered on the stage and a bearded figure, dressed in screaming orange robes walked in and sat cross-legged on the dais. Music, from some thin wailing instrument, made a background noise.
>
> The Swami raised his hand and intoned, Friends – close your eyes. Shut off your senses, withdraw into yourself. We will now travel. ... After twenty minutes, when Chris felt he could bear it no longer, the Swami opened his eyes and said in dulcet tones, Friends, we will now return".
>
> Everyone opened their eyes and quietly began to leave. There was nothing more. The clever Swami had collected a cool thousand dollars for nothing! (p.20).

There is yet another instance narrated with Swiftian sarcasm he has all the claptrap glib on his tongue where the Swamy talks about Kundalini as the

> Key to enlightened and Cosmic Consciousness. The person who succeeds in arousing *Kundalini,* the mystic serpent force that lies coiled at the base of every human beings spine, can develop psychic powers, ecstasies, visions and enlarged consciousness as well as remarkable increase in intellectual power. In a series of five lessons he would teach them how.

The ashram that Dalal acquaints us with next is the one where Chris and Myra stay. That is so that its incongruity with anything genuinely spiritual is easily discernible.

And the ashram in which Rahul is destined to play his own drama is grand and gorgeous - so much so that Rahul could not help feeling that in a way it was rather like a film in which he was the leading star'(p. 27).

The luxuries available at Sukhanand Ashram for Rahul (rechristened as Guru Sukhanand) are another pointer to how spirituality is commercialized in India.

However, *The Inner Door* is not solely or merely a debunking of yoga as such. Yoga has its own merits and efficacies and it can lead man to real God-realisation. And this is brought home to Dalal's readers through the story of Rahul, who is metamorphosed from a low state of pretense into an exalted one of sainthood.'"

Young and handsome, but poor and needy, Rahul drifts, along with his domineering and possessive mother, from his village to Rishikesh, where he hopes to earn his living with the help of his maternal uncle, Swami Jagadish, who runs a small yogashram. But his career, even at the start, is taken charge of by the American couple Chris and Myra who, struck by the boy's film-star-like looks, decide on using him for their own commercial advancement. That is they plan to get Rahul some preliminary training in yoga, open their own ashram, a centre for teaching yoga, and spin easy money. All goes well for quite some time. In his new incarnation Rahul is made popular as Guru Sukhanand and his school is called Sukhanand Ashram, where people who learn yoga are given all modern amenities like posh accommodation, liquor, non-vegetarian food, and even sex. Rahul learns quickly, teaches well and is happy with himself. Arrangements are made for his training in sex with Goldie. All seems to be well, with the popularity of Rahul increasing day by day, and with it the Americans' wealth. His spiritual powers assume sinking dimensions. He even performs miracles. Carl Hanes, the novelist, is so greatly influenced by Rahul's powers that he talks about them gladly and appreciatively. Eventually Rahul slips out of everyone's control and walks out seeking further illumination. Chris, Myra, Ishwar Devi - practically everyone around, realises that Rahul is no longer a pretending godman, but has become a real saint.

As (it) has already been stated, Dalal is as much aware of the pretensions and hypocrisies involved in yoga teaching as she is aware of the genuine dimensions that yogic practices can assume. The idea is important and has been articulated in perhaps the best possible manner by D.R. Sharma:

> Dalal acts neither as an apologist nor a scoffer. Where she indicts the depravity in our saffron-clad prophets, she is equally forthright in her affirmation of the vital discipline of meditation and the yoga. Her novel is not just an expose of our spiritual fetish and moral obliquities, but also and endorsement of that truth which the phony soul searchers can never comprehend. It is this balanced treatment of an endemic theme that sets apart this novel as an enduring piece of creative exploration.[19]

An important point that needs to be made about *The Inner Door* is that it is not a slight performance though not a mighty one. In other words, even though it is an improvement on *Minari* and *The Sisters,* it cannot be said to be free from drawbacks.

Despite the immense potentiality that the novel shows for claiming greatness, the actual result is rather disappointing. We need not shy away from the possible causes just as we should not also be tardy in recognizing the merits.

Admitting that Rahul is the nucleus, Dalal, we may admit has not been totally successful in delineating his character in a convincing manner. That Rahul is a character fraught with possibilities of sainthood is something Dalal has been very particular about hinting even at the beginning. The following extract goes to establish that Rahul is an extraordinary lad:

> Rahul discovered his own method of inducing into his consciousness the intensity moment. He was left in a state of psychic emptiness which was then filled by revelation and a new spiritual certainty.'(p. 85)

As Rahul reaches higher states of consciousness, the river, the sky and the temples around, become for him, a series of vibrations. His love for the hordes of monkeys and compassion for the beggars and all living creatures becomes manifest increasingly. D.R. Sharma views the subtle transformation of Rahul as the core of the novel:

> The theme of self-transcendence is the heart of the novel. Another way to put it would be to call the novel a study in temptation and release -temptation of fame and wealth and the release from these quotidian, satanic concerns.

According to Oscar Wilde,

> Every saint has a past and every sinner has a future.[21]

Perhaps this holds good in the case of Rahul. Aware of a diffused sense of sensual pleasure at the sight of the girls, he yearns for sex with them. Jed takes upon himself the sexual education of Rahul. He encourages Myra and Franoise to initiate Rahul into sex. However, Rahul is repelled by their crude sexual overtures. When Franoise strips herself and begins to stroke Rahul, he is amazed and coolly suggests some 'Asana' for losing her extra fat. Goldie succeeds where others have failed. She is younger and regards sex as nice but not very important. When she performs an Asana with her spine bent backwards and feet stretching above her head touching the ground, Rahul firms up her buttocks and immediately withdraws his hands. Moved by the faint sweetness of her hair, and beneath it another odour' Rahul becomes aware of end tightening of his muscles, a concentration of his mind, rooted down there in his sex.'(pp. 100-101) For Goldie, sex with Rahul is pleasant and passionate. Dalal comments on the Rahul-Goldie affair thus:

> Every encounter with Goldie was a wondering, a melting in delight, in which his (Rahul's) bones and skin and flesh dissolved into honey, his body impaled by rapture. With each successive encounter his desire grew fresh, without satiation, so that the familiar was never the same but always new (pp. 101-102)

Whereas Dalal has been eminently successful in projecting the negative aspects of yoga as it is commercially practiced in India and elsewhere, she does not achieve the same measure of success in delineating its salutary aspects.

It is strange but true that none of Dalal's critics seems to have noticed that of all her novels *The Inner Door* is replete with instances of quiet humour It looks all the more striking because Dalal appears to manage it naturally as it were.

A few illustrations may be noted -

> Both (Rahul and his mother) were carrying bundles, bedding rolls, bags and baskets, *without which no Indian finds it possible to travel,* (p.8) (emphasis added).

Though this appears to be nothing more than an accurate description, what lends a touch of quiet humour to it is Dalal's generalization, so unobtrusively but deftly made.

Just a couple of pages later, we come across one more instance of a similar kind:

> .... Rahul and his mother collected their belongings, the trunks, bedding rolls and small unidentified bundles which they piled around their feet, *in the manner of survivors escaping from some_natural disaster* (p.14) (emphasis added).

It seems to come so naturally to Dalal, what looks like a

mere analogy successfully creates a ripple of a smile without interfering with, but only enhancing, the reader's enjoyment. This may not be surprising in a 'Middle' writer of no mean order, that Nergis Dalal has been.

Either consciously and deliberately or unconsciously and effortlessly, but always cryptically and suggestively, Dalal writes observantly and ironically about men and their strange affairs, attitudes, and practices.

Here is a brief but accurate instance of evocative description of an Indian bus journey –

> The conductor *slammed* the doors shut, blew his whistle piercingly, and the bus started off with much *rattling and shuddering* on its way to Rishikesh. The driver seemed determined to cover the forty and odd miles in the shortest possible time, *swinging* around corners, *leaping* across ditches, and *plunging* through ri\ ulets and streams that poured across the roads from flooded fields. (p. 10) (emphasis added).

The right choice of words (with an eye to comic exaggeration), compression and economy—these have succeeded wonderfully in creating the desired effect.

Something rare and creditable is the novelist's capacity for Popean juxtaposition of the serious and the trivial. Here is an instance in *The Inner Door,* which is so smooth flowing and natural that we cannot fault the reader if he misses it –

> They followed more slowly, Rahul sniffing in the special smell of Rishikesh - a smell compounded of river water, incense and corruption (p. 14).

Dalal can make her reader sit up with surprise and delight by using an extraordinarily apt word instead of opting for some cliché. We have an instance of this where she qualifies the phrase "orange robes" with the adjectivally used "screaming" (p. 20). The effect of such use is that it easily winds the reader's approval and admiration.

Dalal has in her linguistic repertory enough devices of which similies distinguished for their accuracy as well as evocativeness are one. A case in points is -

> He could hear the bus snorting and heaving like a dying monster as it came around the curve and appeared in view (p. 14).

Another instance to show how skilful Dalal is in instituting offbeat but imaginative comparisons is –

> It had rained in the morning but now everything was drying off rapidly as though a giant dryer had been plugged in and turned on to all the little pools and rivulets and streams that collected so quickly after a shower and were now evaporating into the fierce sunshine. (p. 33)

Equally interesting is Dalal's perspicacity which often shows in her arresting world coinage. Her description of the river before dawn as being pearl-touched" (p. 55) is indeed a masterstroke.

We have another instance of Dalal's power of close observation and accurate description when she writes about Hippies thus: Early each morning small groups of Hippies appeared, all of them quite obviously foreign, but *in a state of dirtiness difficult to describe* (p. 70) (emphasis added). The Hippie not described at length only because they are superlatively dirty - or indescribably so.

We have several instances scattered all through the novel to show that Dalal's knowledge of yoga is wide, deep, and authentic too. The following passage relating to a description of Chakras illustrates the point:

> Now turn your minds eye on the six *Chakras*. You have all learnt their positions, but if any of you have trouble please consult the chart in front of you, hanging on the wall there. Concentrate first on the *Mulahadra Chakra*. Relax, let yourself go soft, there should be no tenseness anywhere. Now bring your mind to the *Swadishthana Chakra* and relax your legs.

> Now the *Manipura Chakra,* relax the abdominal area, front and back. Concentrate, concentrate. Now into the *Ahuhala Chakra,* the heart area, up into the neck into the *Vishuddha Chakra.* and then bring your consciousness, your minds eye into its resting place between the eyebrows into the *Ajna Chakra.* Keep it there, relax, enjoy the bliss of the peaceful. *OM ! Shanti, Shanti, Shanti OM.* (p. 41).

Unless one is very careful, one is likely to miss the several instances of Dalal's mastery of the telling phrase, of evocative description, aptness of analogy, and similar other verbal felicities which together make for a calculated.

Early on in the novel we have the following description of Rahul's poverty and consequent hunger—all done so precisely and unsentimentally:

> Without turning his head, Rahul sniffed up the savoury smell of food. He realised again how hungry he was. He had eaten nothing but a banana this morning before leaving. He was always hungry. One of the miseries of having so little money was that he was eternally hungry. His mother has packed some cold chapattis and dal in a stainless steel box for their lunch, but now he felt a touch on his shoulder and turning, found Myra offering him a whole packet of sandwiches (p.11).

Dalal can insert a generalization here and a generalization there generalizations which are contextually relevant, and which you may take for what they are worth:

> In India there are always people who have time to stand and stare. Crowds collect magically for any untoward event, evidently prepared to stand around endlessly and gape, as though there was nothing in life more important than to watch (p. 69).

Though it can be said without much fear of contradiction that Nergis Dalal's third novel *The Inner Door* is better than either of her earlier novels, *Minari* and *The Sisters,* to place it on a high pedestal and prophesy, as D.R. Sharma does, that if Dalal could come out with one more novel like *The Inner Door* her place in the world of Indian English fictionists would be secure, is not a proposition that might find universal acceptance.[22] However, it needs to be admitted that *The Inner Door* is less loosely knit and better structured than any of Dalal's other novels and establishes better claims to acclaim than her earlier ones.

One notices the theme of East-West encounter pervading the novel. Dalal's sketch of the East is presented through diverse view-points. Swami Ramananda who has lectured extensively in New York offers his Indian Ashram for instruction in Inner-Life Meditation'. This has been for some time a model for Rahul who is impressed by its luxurious catering to Western tastes. During an early rehearsal Rahul demonstrates for Ramananda and others his practice of Hata-Yoga but, as it turns out, Ramananda has acquired certain powers like materializing a gold ring out of air. Rahul's is not on Ramananda's path.

Another version of the East is offered through Rahul's uncle, Swami Jagdish. Finding his sister and nephew with the Stewarts, Jagdish is elated at the prospect of wealth to be got through Chris's plans. The materialism of the West represented by Myra and Chris finds its echo in Jagdish. Even Rahul's mother is not immune to the lure of wealth for, though she suspects that Rahul has an ongoing affair with Goldie, she remains silent. Ironically, while the so called spiritual gurus like Ramananda and Jagdish cannot recognise Rahul's transformation, it is his illiterate mother, alone among all the Indians, who bows and touches the feet of Rahul. But in the end she too regrets that Rahul had not been corrupted early enough. Jed, Goldie and Duncan among the Westerners are truly touched by Rahul's spirituality.

In Dalal's version of the East-West encounter, the Westerners seek to cast the East in their own mould. In reality, the East itself is a crude mixture. As Dalal describes Rishkesh:

> The spurious and the genuine existed here side by side and often it was difficult to make out the difference, since truth and falsehood also existed here as illusions inside the mind and correct Drishti was possible only for the enlightened (p.16).

The ashram offers the comforts of a five-star hotel. Its accent on sex in yoga and secret provision for liquors and non-vegetarian food are sure indications of the western model.

While Dalal's *The Inner Door* deals with Rahul's search for selfhood, another powerful novel of hers, viz. *The Girls from Overseas* concerns itself with the sense of existential alienation of the five *Girls from overseas.*[24] Despite their marriages to well-placed professionals – Jane's marriage to Dr. Sunil Kumar, a promising surgeon, Louise's marriage to Dinesh, an Engineering graduate from Stanford, Michelle's and Gertrude's marriage to successful military officers—Generals Raj Varma and George Das respectively, and Sandy's marriage to Dilip Singh, kin to royalty—these 'girls' are unable to identify with, or relate to, their Indian ethos.

THE GIRLS FROM OVERSEAS

It is surprising to note that foreign women in Indian English Fiction experience a sense of strangeness and unreality and live as visitors from another planet altogether. Meena Shirwadkar rightly observes:

> Their world is built round clubs, estates, parties at hill stations, their occupations, besides gossip, would be attending parties, dances, flirting and frivolity. [25]

These lines show how the women from abroad lead a life of alienation, Prof. M.K. Naik observes:

> The stock theme of East-West encounter is treated in *The Girls from Overseas.* [26]

The truth is that Mrs. Dalal emphasizes the frustration and despair and the vacuity of the inner lives, of the foreign women. Pointing out the relevance of the displacement of the girls's to their characterization, O.P. Bhatnagar comments thus:

> The well-known technique initiated by Henry James in English Fiction of drawing characters away from narrow securities and displacing them from their environment and studying their reactions has been successfully tried here."[27]

In their attempts to preserve their foreign identity, the foreign women form a loose group and meet at coffee parties in their homes by turns. The novel is chiefly built round these parties and their social celebrations.

The Girls from Overseas are the victims of their extra native cultural affiliation and the resultant culturally-conditioned perception. In this sense, they cannot escape from their background. Their response to India is that of ethno-centrism, a tendency of all white peoples' to judge others by ones own values and beliefs,' which only underlines Dalal's assertion that a dividing line separates the two cultures' and can never be overcome.'(p. 184) It is not surprising then, that on their advent and subsequent residence in India, they experience an identity crisis'(p. 146) which intensifies their sense of alienation. Conscious as they are of their white racial superiority they insulate themselves from the natives of India. They trust only their own kind, kindred souls like Jason Skinner, to whom they complain about their husbands, and relations and sometimes slept with him.'(p. 13) Steeped in antipathy towards India, they live insulated in their modernised houses spending their time in shopping - spreas and also in conjuring up beauty of the foreign gardens. To put it in a nutshell, these women face a cultural encounter and existential query.[28]

D.R. Sharma, who is probably the most perceptive of Dalal's critics sanguinely prognosticated that if the writer could produce another novel of the artistic calibre of *The Inner Door,* her name would find a permanent niche in the temple of Indian English letters." It is sad but true that Dalal's last latest novel, *The Girls from Overseas* clearly belies his expectations. It not only fails to excel *The Inner Door* but is decidedly inferior to it.

Sarala Barnabas, who has written rather extensively, though not always quite perceptively, seems to hit the nail right on the head when she defines the theme of *The Girls from Overseas* as the Kiplingian idea of the impossibility of meeting of the East and the West.[30]

The primary motivating force that has shaped the *Girls from Overseas* is Dalal's conviction that inter-cultural marital alliances are fraught with perennial problems. In order to prove this, Dalal portrays five foreign girls' from four different nations, France, U.K., U.S.A. and Canada - married unhappily to Indian men. These girls are plunged into despair as a consequence of the cultural disparity between them and their husbands. They find succor neither in their native countries nor in the countries, they have adopted. We would not be wrong if we described them as nowhere women" who are victims of existential angst, confusion and misery. It should also be possible to describe them as hollow women."

During the course of the novel we find that Indians receive castigation from Dalal as much as the foreigners. Louise, Michelle, Sandy, Jane and Gertrude - all stationed in Dehra Dun—meet once a week at one or other of their houses, ostensibly for coffee, but in reality to talk about their husbands, children, in-laws, and various problems they encounter because they are foreigners. "Their weekly meetings were safety valves-analysts couch and confessional, at one and the same time." (p. 7).

We may begin with Michelle, the French woman married to General Raj, who has, despite her forty-year-long stay in India, repelled all Indian influence and retained her identity. "Her surroundings, her children, even her husband, seemed to have adapted themselves to Michelle not she to them. Even her English, after all these years, was faintly accented" (p.7) Michelle who has been caricatured as an elephant in miniature, believes that in India it is difficult to get anything pure. In this country everything is adulterated'(p. 23).

Jane and Sunil constitute another pair unhappily yoked together. Jane's repugnance for India and all things Indian appears to be hereditary. Her mother hated Indians so heartily that she was utterly against her daughter's marriage with an Indian, "I would rather you were dead than married to an Indian." (p. 16).

But, then, Jane has additional reasons for her hearty dislike of India. She hates her mother-in-law as well as her sister-in-law. She believes that Indian mothers are abnormally possessive of their sons. Patently Jane only looks at her mother-in-law with jaundiced eyes. For instance, the simple fact of a mother feeding her son lovingly appears objectionable to her. She says:

> She (Jane's mother-in-law) sits in the kitchen frying up things for Sunil to stuff himself on when he gets home in the evening, and he has put on weight, thanks to her. She picks up a pakora or a sweet and puts it into his mouth with her fingers. It is positively incestuous. They should do a psychoanalytical study of Indian mothers. I am sure they all have this secret desire to sleep with their sons (p. 15).

That is clearly going too far. Well, to continue with Indian mothers-in-law and sisters in-law, on the other hand, are to blame too because they are incapable of even a slight degree of accommodation and adjustment. They treat their daughter-in-law as an outsider. That is clearly to be seen in the case of Jane.

> Both (the mother-in-law and the sister-in-law) doted on Sunil and resented Jane, the outsider, who had usurped the place they had reserved for a nice little Indian bride who would have no needs or desires of her own, who would put up with Sunil no matter what he did, who would cook, keep house, do as she was told, listen to every one's problems and produce babies, preferably sons, at regular intervals (p.84).

However, Indians are not altogether blemishless and they can irritate any sensitive individual with even a modicum of self-respect. Here is a description of the uncouth behaviour of some of the so-called respectable people of India at the time of Holi:

> Catching hold other Aroon poured dark red powder in a stream over her head, rubbing it roughly with his fingers and drawing his smeared hand down her body, pressing breasts, belly, thighs with probing, hard fingers Jane jerked back, startled and annoyed. Savitri came up, spray in her hand and with a high, silly laugh, drenched Jane from head to toe with coloured water, concentrating on her face. Jane's eyes smarted and colour tricked into her mouth. "Here, that's enough", she said, but they were past listening. One by one, tolal -strangers

> came up and pressed their coloured hands over her body, poured ink-like water over her hair and dusted coloured powder, shining with bits of mica, over her clothes. She tried to run away but they refused to let her go, and all the time there was the high, silly laughter. Sunil tried to rescue her and was picked up bodily and flung into the pond. One of the men lifted Jane and swung her to and fro, while the others stood around laughing and giggling. She was crying with fright, temper and rage—but no one noticed her tears. (p.153).

Jane is naturally so hurt that she bursts forth in disgust mixed with hurt and anger: "Savages, barbarians that's what they are" (p. 153).

Consider the authorial comments in this regard "All Indians were like glaciers she felt-civilized on the surface but deep down, beneath the surface, they were violent savages." (p. 154).

It is difficult to say how far Dalal would associate herself with this line of thinking. Is she here holding a camera to the innermost thoughts of the characters only as an omniscient author?

Not that Jane is an angel - far from that. She is flippant as well irritable. And, like the rest of the foreign girls in the novel, Jane cannot boast of a spotless character. Sleeping with Jason had been a pleasurable experience that she now looked back upon as the only perfect sexual relation she had ever had [p 25).

It is evident that the match between Jane and Sunil was only a misalliance. Mutual recrimination can never solve marital problems. A successful marriage needs mutual tolerance and understanding and considerable adjustment. And that is precisely what is wanting in these girls and their mates.

The following lines "put the finger" on where exactly the cause of the couples' misery and unhappiness lay. "She

(Jane) wondered why, if she must marry, she had to pick on a foreigner, whose culture was totally different from hers and whose attitude towards life was shaped by that culture" (p. 15).

The next ill-assorted pair is that of Louise and Dinesh.

Louise, a Canadian, a well paid stenographer, despite her love for her husband, Dinesh, a Stanford – trained Engineer, finds it difficult to adjust herself to her new surroundings in India. Her mother-in-law in particular is a constant irritant with her slovenly habits and her complaint that Sonia, her grand- daughter, has not inherited the fair complexion of her mother. The authorial comments on the situation clearly bring out the mother-in-laws' attitude:

> At first Dinesh's mother had been upset at the colour of Sonia's skin. She had hoped (it was one of the things that made marrying a foreigner acceptable) that the child would be very fair, white, like her mother. Indians have this curious prejudice about a fair skin which is supposed to denote descent from the civilized Aryan invaders from the north, while a dark skin meant descent from primitive tribes who had been pushed into jungles or fled south. The advertisements in the matrimonial columns always specified a fair bride, as though fairness had something more finely and delicately adjusted in it, more superior. Two hundred years of colonial rule had done nothing to diminish tins prejudice. (pp. 19-20).

Dinesh's people at home realize that it is difficult for them to make Louise mend her ways, and so, they themselves come round and try to adjust themselves to the foreigner. Yet, Louise finds that India is too much for her to accept. She is young and full of ideals, she is truly in love with Dinesh, adores her small daughter Sonia, but finds India hard.

Yet another infertile marital union relates to Sandy and Dilip Singh. How can happiness result from a wedlock between a woman who believes that her marriage has been a mistake and a man who is impotent?

Sandy is an outspoken extrovert American who is married to Dilip, a rich jeweller. One can easily guess what a hopeless alliance it is when one is given to understand that the lady is thinking of divorce after just a week of her wedding.

Through reputed to be "a ladies' man", Dilip is said to be totally impotent so far as his wife is concerned. What is disconcerting is that Sandy had enjoyed having Jason as friend and lover too" (p. 27) even as she loved all the comforts Dilip could give her. It is a kind of love-hate relationship that persists in the case of this couple. The wife is unfaithful and the husband is aware of this fact - nay, it is much more than that, he would not even be disturbed by it. Dilip makes this explicit:

> My dear Sandy. Don't be naïve. I knew you were having an affair with him I didn't object. For some reason we don't seem to click on the sexual plane. I find you slightly intimidating and for me a woman has to be pliant, submissive - even - subservient - to be sexually exciting. You are a very strong personality and you seem to pour out vibrations which clash with my own, especially, in intimate moments (p.143).

The author clinches the issue thus; perhaps they had both been looking for an escape route, and not love."(p. 147). If this wedding between Sandy and Dilip, a failure from the beginning" (p. 147) has not totally disintegrated they owe it perhaps to Sandy's mother-in-law, Mataji, who is one of the most lovable characters created by Dalal.

The last unhappy couple presented by Dalal is that of Gertrude and George Das. That again is a marriage of convenience rather than love. Gertrude married Das only 'to get away from a very dull life in a small town' (p. 39). A boozer and womanizer, Das neglects his wife so badly that the marriage is "a disaster, it seems, from the very beginning" (p. 39). The bitterness between the couple gets thick when their sick child died because the husband was indifferent and neglectful.

Gertrude vehemently refuses to identify herself with the country of her adoption. She tells the other foreign girls.[7]

> I don't know what has got into all of you. What's the matter with you? Why should we identify with this country when each one of us has been very careful to preserve a separate identity, retain British or American passports and refused to apply for Indian citizenshi.p (p. 88).

She says further:

> ...as for identifying with this country on the contrary. I have done everything possible to retain my separateness. I have no desire at all to merge with a people who are at least a 100 years behind the times.... (p. 89).

Gertrude even takes to the study and practice of witchcraft, achieves (or thinks, she has achieved) some success, and dies miserably of a heart attack.

Though our chief concern is with the five foregoing ill-matched pairs, one or two minor characters in the novel also claim our attention.

Globe-trotting Jason Skinner, ostensibly working for the UNO, is a close friend, and lover of all the foreign girls. In fact he is their great comforter. As the novelist describes:

> Jason Skinner had somehow come to mean a great deal to each one of them. He was their safety valve - confidante, accomplice. His job with the United Nations took him on trips all over the world every few months or oftener, from where he brought back for them bottles of Scotch, vodka, cherry brandy, perfumes, cosmetics, cigarettes and even clothes. They just told him what it was they wanted, and like a perennial Santa Claus, lie turned up with everything. He was none of those unattached males of indeterminate age, who shed their not inconsiderable charm on all women, old or young. He genuinely liked women and he was also extremely good-natured. He liked to please people and it was by pure accident that he found himself in the special position that he occupied today, vis-a-vis the girls (pp. 11-12).

Further -

> They confided in him, complained about husbands and relations, and sometimes, slept with him He was their very special friend, a foreigner like themselves, with whom they were safe, at case.... None of them questioned his relationship with the others. They guarded their own, and were content that it did not collide with that of the others (p. 13).

But, then, Jason is not to be satisfied with this situation. He marries Maya, a reputed dancer and shocks all the five girls almost out of their wits.

Towards the end of the novel we are given to see the true colours of Jason, who is a smuggler, very much wanted by the police and hunted by them.

Dalal seems to have bestowed all her loving care on the creation of Mataji - perhaps the noblest character in the novel. Despite all the suffering she has herself had to undergo in the initial stages of her married life, she reveals herself as a character with—true blue blood as we observe her relations with the other characters.

Two important points that emerge from a close study of the novel are marital alliances between Indians and foreigners seldom have a chance of flourishing because of the cultural disparities which are too strong to be easily dissolved, and two, b) Dalal has riddled the novel with too many generalizations which may or may not be true, or may only be partial truths.

In the foregoing pages we have had a glimpse of the former point, and now we may try to have a look at the latter one.

Had characters, loose ends of stories, dearth of that white-hot creative imagination which is the *sine qua non* of a great work of art... these are some of the charges that may be levelled against Dalal's longer fiction in general and *The Girls from Overseas* in particular. However there is no question of doubting the sincerity of the author's central purpose in the novel— in this case we ought to take cognizance of Dalal's vision and understanding of some of the basic attitudes of both Indians and foreigners which characterize their behaviour - mutually and otherwise too. We may or may not always agree with Dalal but there is no escape from accepting her sincerity.

The novel offers several instances of Dalal's criticism of India and Indians, offered by Dalal herself in the capacity of author or by the characters in the novel, and we may examine some of them, if not all.

Let us take a simple observation that Dalal makes about Indian women's strange ways of dressing:

> Indian women tended either to overdress or slop around the house untidily in housecoats or pyjamas (p.28).

This is by no means flattering to our women, but Dalal's observation here seems to be unbiased and accurate, though there may be exceptions but exceptions only prove the rule rather than refute it.

Look at this withering comment of Michelle on the probity of Indian merchants. "In this country everything is adulterated" (p.23). Without bothering to insist on statistical evidence, one may tend to agree with the statement though it comes from a foreigner. Again, there may be exceptions.

Mark these words of Gertrude about the enormous violence and cruelty that Indians are capable of:

> All their (Indians) Western sophistication is surface deep and underneath they are a violent people with violent emotions. Every moment that I am outside of my house I am assailed with this violence, this filth, this cruelty to their own kind as

> well as to animals. They enjoy cruelty. Twisting the tails and testicles of bulls — beating and starving small ponies and donkeys – tying up pet dogs all day in the sun or leaving them on terraces where they can't run about. They are a savage people and don't tell me about their ancient civilization. We are like prisoners who must stay forever in this jail. I have no wish to identify with this country, this people. I despise them. Indeed I sometimes feel I detest them. (p. 89).

In the light of foregoing excerpt, it is possible to accuse Dalal of viewing the Indian situation with jaundiced eyes. In a way she reminds us of Naipaul. Her picture of an Indian beggar is particularly reminiscent of Naipaul:

> He sat on a dirty bit of cloth with an empty tin in front of him to which was attached, by a string, two small bells of the kind that cattle wear around their necks. In his left hand he held some sort of cymbals. Without a moments pause, his blind eyes turned up to the sky, he clashed the cymbals, pulled the bells and turned his head incessantly from side to side. It was gruesome, horrible, made more so by the indifference of the passers - by who rarely even glanced at him. Once in a while someone would stop and drop a coin into the box but the beggar made no sign of acknowledgement. For a moment only the bells were put down, the coin scooped up and then again the bizarre spectacle continued (pp.162—163).

She repeatedly comments on the duplicity embedded in the Indian character so far as their talk of *ahimsa* vis-à-vis their practice of cruelty in respect of animals:

> No, she (Louise) would never understand them, a people dedicated to ahimsa, who nevertheless behaved with a chilling cruelly to animals (p 120)

Look at the way dogs are treated by Indians. In the words of Louise;

> Unfortunately in this country, most dogs are kept like that – miserable brutes who are never allowed to run free – never permitted to enter the house. Next door to us, two beautiful alsations are permanently confined to the terrace where they bark their hearts out without anyone paying the slightest attention to them (p. 139).

Gertrude too feels that way;

> Like all foreigners, Gertrude could never understand how any people claiming to believe in ahimsa, could be so unbelievably cruel to animals. It was a constant heartache for her to see the abandoned puppies, the thin and starving bitches, the overloaded bullock carts and the small, starved tonga ponies that were everywhere (p. 105).

Most of the time marriage is seen in the novel as a covenant of convenience rather than a holy sacrament. Marriage for money, marriage for social status, marriage for sex .... that is how it is with the girls' and their men. The result is therefore expectedly unpleasant. And this is clear from the fact that none of the five 'girls' treats marriage with the seriousness it deserves; none of them is faithful; and none of them is really happy. No marriage is 'all plain sailing', adultery is very common, and divorce is respectably round the corner. Consider the following lines:

> What did anyone ever know of other people's marriages? Perhaps all couples were basically hostile to each other and there was no such thing as a happy marriage. Perhaps unhappiness, hostility were the absolutely infallible conditions of any marriage (p.147).

Dalal thus may look hopelessly cynical in her attitude to marriage, but we should remember that it is all symptomatic of a rotting society and not a universal situation. Dalal's intention is to paint the picture of a certain class of people and in this we must say she is faithful and successful.

Though on the whole *The Girls from Overseas* is not a total artistic tour deforce, it clearly proves that Dalal has an intimate knowledge of people and the problems she deals with. Also, sometimes, though not always, her language glows, sparkles and allures our attention. Take, for instance, the following examples:

> She (Sonia) made it into a song, skipping up and down and

> the dog lolled its tongue out as though laughing, and nibbled her ears affectionately.

That is an instance of a perfect match between sense and sound.

> Dalal's language when it refers to the dancer Maya flitting about like an orange bird, hair swirling, hardly seeming to touch the floor as she walked (p. 33).

Another instance of Dalal's sensitive use of language is to be seen in her description of Simba, Sonia's pup, as "the sleeping ball of fur" (p. 60).

Yet another illustration of Dalal's ability to use language imaginatively is seen in the following extract;

> The air poured down from the mountains and felt cool on their faces. Everything was fresh in the crystal air. A flower blew loose from its stalk and hovered and became a butterfly that floated past the heads into the shining sunlight (p.110).

Such poetical touches sprinkle the narrative with light and colour all through.

The thematic freshness of the novel, no doubt, is commendable.

The Girls from Overseas is very unique in its handling of the East-West encounter, as Bhatnagar rightly points out: "Of all the novels written on this theme this is the most cool and objective statement of the East-West confrontation in family affairs". [31] As reflected in the action highlighting the theme of East-West encounter, Sandy's characterisation has a significance far above that of others. This can be explained by her being the vehicle through which the benign influence of Mataji and the sinister impact of Vikram are brought into operation. What distinguishes her from the other girls is her experimental and pragmatic approach to making a success of marriage, as if working over a doctoral thesis. While others are repelled by India and complain, she tries to trace the cause of the disturbance intellectually. Some of her revealing observations may be cited: the mental climate of a place could be as foreign as the physical terrain. Centuries of prejudice, presupposition and tradition had resulted in the society that responded to living with corrupting conventions and distorting preconceptions."(pp.56-57). She correctly compares her situation to that of a wanderer in a strange world with a compass having no magnetic pole. Her emotional fervour is reflected in her insistence upon participating in Holi against the advice and warning of Arun and Dilip.

Michelle too is capable of a certain degree of intellectual analysis. However, her perceptions do not have a direct relevance unlike Sandy's. Michelle philosophizes about the function of the mind which like a highly complex computer card with a constant feedback, (is) influenced by every thought and impression so that one observed, constantly from a certain, predesigned angle" (p. 101). The characterizations of Sandy and Michelle furnish the psychological base from which the theme of East-West encounter is explored in the novel.

In conclusion we may say that Nergis Dalal's four novels project the theme of alienation along with other issues that arise incidentally and have been discussed in the analysis done of the novels in this chapter. To repeat, Nergis Dalal is not a "committed" writer, true however the following concerns standout in each of her novels a) alienation, b) marriage, c) east-west encounter, and d) human relations. While her first novel *Minari* depicts the complex emotions, passions and psychological tensions in the world of Anita, her second novel *The Sisters* concerns itself with Rita's search for meaning. Her third novel *The Inner Door* comes before us as a natural sequel to *The Sisters* as it deals with Rahul who assumes several roles in his quest for selfhood. Her next novel, *The Girls from Overseas* very grippingly depicts the identity crisis faced by the *Girls from* abroad. From *Minari* to *The Girls from Overseas* Dalal stretches her imaginative canvas to present a realistic portrayal of the protagonists' feelings of alienation. It is in marriage that this feeling of alienation is mostly experienced. In her own words one can see in these four novels the writer's heightened responsiveness of the world".

REFERENCES

1. Nergis Dalal, "On How I Became a Writer", in R.K. Dhwan, (ed.), *Indian Women Novelists,* New Delhi: Prestige, 1995, p. 10
2. O.P. Bhatnagar, "Nergis Dalal;" in Madhusudhan Prasad (ed.) *Indian Women Novelists,* New Delhi: Sterling Publishers, 1982, p. 133
3. Nergis Dalal, *Minari,* New Delhi: Orient Paperbacks, 1967.
4. M.K. Naik, *A History of Indian English Literature,* New Delhi: Sahitya Akademi, 1982, p. 243.
5. Novy Kapadia, "The Theme of Selfhood in Nergis Dalal's *Minari* and *The Inner Door,*" *Indian Women Novelists,* p. 25.
6. O.P. Bhalnagar, "Nergis Dalal;" in Madhusudhan Prasad (ed.), *Indian Women Novelists,* New Delhi: Sterling Publishers, 1982, p.133.
7. V.S. Naipaul, *A House for Mr. Biswas,* London: Andre Deutsch, 1961.
8. *Ibid.,* p. 40.
9. Harold Barrat, "The Liberated Self: V.S. Naipaul's Autobiography and Fiction," *The Literary Half Yearly,* Vol. 30, No.1, 1989, p. 145.
10. Vasant A. Shahane, "The Symbol of the House in V.S. Naipaul's Early Novels," *Osmania Journal of English Studies,* 1982, p. 51.
11. Nergis Dalal, *The Sisters,* New Delhi: Hind Pocket Books, 1973.
12. M.K. Naik, *A History of Indo-English Literature,* p. 243.
13. O.P. Bhatnagar, "Nergis Dalal", in Madhusudhan Prasad (ed.), *Indian Women Novelists,* New Delhi: sterling publishers, 1982, p. 134
14. *Ibid.,* p. 138.
15. M.K. Naik, p. 243.

16. Nergis Dalal, *The Inner Door,* New Delhi: Orient Longman, 1976.
17. O.P. Bhatnagar, Nergis Dalal, in Madhusudhan Prasad (ed.) *Indian Women Novelists,* New Delhi: Sterling Publishers, 1982, p. 138.
18. Ramesh Srivastava, "From Caterpiller to Butterfly: Stages in Rahul's metamorphosis to Sainthood", *Recent Indian Fiction in English,* Berielly: Prakash Book Depot, 1983, p. 265
19. D.R. Sharma, "The Creative Art of Nergis Dalal," *Journal of Indian Writing in English,* Vol. 5, No. 1, Jan 1977, p. 141.
20. *Ibid.,* p. 142.
21. Oscar Wilde, *A Woman of No Importance,* p. III.
22. D.R. Sharma, *op. cit.,* p. 142.
23. Nergis Dalal, *The Girls from Overseas,* New Delhi: Hind Pocket Books, 1979.
24. Ferheiz C. Bharucha, "Nergis Dalal's *The Girls from Overseas:* A Cultural Encounter and Existential Query," *Indian Women Novelists,* p. 109.
25. Meena Shirwadkar, *Image of Women in Indo-Anglian Fiction,* New Delhi: Sterling, 1979, p. 8.
26. M.K. Naik, p. 243.
27. O.P. Bhatnagar, Nergis Dalal, *Indian Women Novelists,* ed. Madhusudhan Prasad, New Delhi: Sterling Publishers, 1982, p. 143.
28. Ferheiz C. Bharucha, Nergis Dalal's *The Girls from Overseas",* *Indian Women Novelists,* New Delhi, 1982, p. 109.
29. D.R. Sharma, "The Creative Art of Nergis Dalal", *Journal of Indian Writing in English,* Vol. g, No. 1, Jan 1977, p. 28.
30. See Sarala Barnabas, Nergis Dalal's *The Girls from Overseas* and Ruth Prawar Jhabvala's, *A Backward Place,* in *Indian Women Novelists,* New Delhi, Prestige, p. 82
31. O.P. Bhatanagar, "Nergis Dalal", in Madhusudhan Prasad (ed.) *Indian Women Novelists,* New Delhi: Sterling Publishers, 1982, p.149

4

Nergis Dalal's Short Stories

THE NUDE

As a literary form the short story may be the most recent in the evolution of literature types but,

> The brief story is probably as old as human imagination. Its recorded history dates back even earlier than the semi-fictional gems of the early Hindus, Hebrews and Buddhists.[1]

From very early days man has taken delight in telling stories and listening to stories. Crude and elementary but highly effective short stories are found in the Old Testament in the form of parables told by Jesus. The early Anglo-Saxon stories from Bede to Beowolf dealt with miracles, wars and the lives of saints. We also find in them a reflective mood probing into human nature. Along with Chaucer we may name Gower, Ludgate and others in whose verse we find a developing conception of the short story.

In the 17th century we see a few character books' in which the story form emerges from the essay. The 18th century magazines, like *Gentleman's Magazine, The Spectator, The Tatler* etc., carried character essays. Daniel Defoe's *Robinson Crusoe* deals with a story depicting realistically the society around him. In the 19th century Hannah More's stories served a moral purpose. Maria Edgeworth's, *The Moral Tales* and *Popular Tales* dealt with varied themes. Walter Scott also wrote quite a few short stories. The beginning of the 19th century saw an unprecedented rise in the number of writers in England as well as in America. With rapid industrialization people had little patience to read thick novels. The demand for short stories increased resulting in the publication of hundreds of short stories on both sides of the Atlantic.

It was Edgar Allan Poe who provided the first critical axioms for judging the merit of a short story. According to him.

> A short story is a prose narrative requiring from half an hour to one or two hours in its perusal.

So we can possibly say that the short story is a prose narrative that can be read in half an hour to one or two hours at a single sitting. It is a narrative with greater emphasis on plot and with freer handling of time sequence.

A short story should confine itself to a single incident. It should concentrate its attention on a particular aspect of a character and create a vivid impression. Sometimes, skillful short story writers describe more than one incident. For example, in Washington Irving's *"Ripvan Winkle"*, we see a tale of a life time.

A short story should have unity of motive, purpose and impression. It should contain only one informing idea, the idea being worked out to its logical conclusion, with the singleness of aim and directness of method. Poe's *The Cask of Amontillado* is a case in point. In a novel, there can be many threads and the central organising principle may be difficult to find, but it is not so in a short story. The singleness of aim and the singleness of purpose are two very important canons by which the value of a short story is judged. One of the principal difficulties of writing a short story is the attainment of unity. Therefore, the short story asks for perfection of workmanship. This is clear from Poe's comments in his review of Hawthorne's *Twice Old Tales*. 'A skilful literary artist having conceived, with deliberate care, a certain unique or single effect to be wrought out, invites such incidents... so many best aid him in establishing the preconceived effect. If his very initial sentence tends not to bring this out then he has failed in his first step. In the whole composition there should be no word written, of which the tendency, direct or indirect, is not to the one pre-established. And by such means, with care and skill, a picture is at length painted which leaves in the mind of him who contemplates it with kindred art, a sense of the fullest satisfaction. The idea of the tale has been presented, unblemished, because undisturbed, and this is an end unattainable by a novel.[3]

A good short story should exclude all unnecessary details. Any incident or character that does not further the single effect desired must be omitted. Usually it does not allow padding. A story may deal with any motive or material. As A.E. Bates rightly says:

> The range of a short story can be anything from a prose poem without plot or character to the analysis of the most complex human emotions, and that it can deal with any subject from the death of a horse, the loss of a clock to a girl's first love affair.[4]

Washington's Irvings's *The Stout Gentleman*' has a purely whimsical theme. Thus, the short story has an immense range in respect of theme.

> A dramatic incident or situation, a telling scene, a closely coordinated series of events, a phase of a character, a bit of experience, an aspect of life, moral problem— any of these, and innumerable other motives may be made the nucleus of a thoroughly satisfactory story. [5]

It is pertinent to go into a brief history of the short story both in the west and in the East.

Various writers in the West have contributed to the growth and development of the short story. Edgar Allan Poe, Hawthorne, O. Henry, Faulkner are a few American writers who contributed solidly to the flourishing literary form of short story. Edgar Allan Poe is mainly concerned with terror and sadness in his short stories. In such pieces as *'The Murder in the Rue Morgue'* (1841) and *'The Raven'* (1845) he made a fusion of the mysterious and the macabre. O. Henry, in his short stories, depicted the lives of ordinary people in New York City. His stories successfully made use of the element of co-incidence and suspense. His stories of adventure in South-West America and Central America became very popular among the readers. His book *Cabbages and Kings* depicted fantastic characters against the exotic Honduran background. His imagination earned him away from the material world into a dream land. In addition to Poe and O. Henry, Jack O. London and William Faulkner contributed solidly to the growth of the short story in America.

In Britain, Somerset Maugham appeared as a major short-story writer in 1898. *'James Joyce'*, with the publication of *Dubliners' rose* as a solid writer of short stories. D.H. Lawrence published a large number of short stories between 1930-1934. H.G. Wells is known for his collection of short stories: *The Stolen Bacillus and Other Incidents.* Henry James also lent a hand to the development of the short stories are complicated and complex.

The short story in India is rather deeply rooted, in our native tradition... This tradition is unquestionably as old as Indian society and culture. According to C.V. Venugopal,

> The Indian tale existed broadly in two forms namely the fable and the popular tale or the folk tale. [7]

The ancient Indian tradition took broadly two forms- the fable and the popular tale or the folk tale. The fable form is best exemplified in the tales of *Panchatantra as* well as *Jataka Tales, Bruhath Kathamanjari,* and *Katha Sarithsagara.* Most of these are animal fables in which the characters are animals symbolizing human beings. These fables are more akin to the modern short story than the popular tale of ancient India.

Both the ancient Indian fable and the ancient Indian popular tale have helped the Indian short story writer in English in giving his story a definite shape. The Indian short story in English tried a synthesis of the salient features of both the fable and the popular tale. The fable and the popular tale have also this feature, viz. of whetting the curiosity of the reader by imparting to him some useful knowledge in a most interesting way. There has been no instance of an Indian who has not taken an interest in these at some time or the other.

By the second half of the 19th century, English literature had its impact on Indian writing in English. Prose works were attempted and newer forms like lyric, novel, short story began to appear in Indian languages. By the end of the century, short stories in the English language itself began to be written by Indian writers. The modern Indian short story in English is a synthesis of the age old cultural traditions of India and the modern trends of realism and humanism. This helped the Indian writer to project the image of India as it really is, its greatness and smallness, its cities and its villages, its men and its women, its religion and superstitions, its wisdom and its ignorance.[8]

It was in 1898 that the first collection of short stories was published by Kamala Sathinandan in her *Indian Christian Life.* At the beginning of the 20th century. Cornelia Sorabji, a Parsi woman, published her four collections of short stories namely – *'Love and life Behind the Purdah'* (1901), *Sunbabies: Studies in Child Life of India* (1904), *Between the Twilights*

(1908). *Indian Tales of the Great Ones Among Men Women and Blind People* (1916). These are stories depicting mostly Hindu life in those days. These are generally sympathetic in tone, with an undercurrent of social reform and are narrated in a leisurely Victorian manner.[9]

Manjeri S. Iswaran is one of the early Indian writers of the short story. His stories are primarily concerned with lower middle class life *Sea Shells, The Cradle and Immersion* are some of his representative stories that deal with the theme of love, the consequences of the World Wars and the national movement.

K.S. Venkat Ramani is another writer, who in his *Jaladharana and Other Stories,* exposes the more conspicuous social evils prevailing in the society of his times. In his stories, he presents South Indian life both in its traditionally conservative and its dynamic modern aspects with convincing sincerity and fascinating power. His studies and interpretations are charged with sympathy, understanding and imagination and range over a wide various fields.

K. Nagarajan, with his single volume of short stories entitled *Cold Rice,* rose to prominence as a short story writer. He manipulates the story in such a way that the story ends tragically or even indeterminately. The life he portrays in his stories is never unreal. Thus, to venture a generalisation, the early writers working in the area of short story are for the most part, deficient in originality of conception and depth of characterization.

In the mid 20th century, the Indian English short story came into prominence at the hands of three Big writers—Mulk Raj Anand, Raja Rao and R.K. Narayan. While Anand presents in his stories the dirt and squalor, superstitions and blind adherence to tradition in Indian society. Raja Rao discusses social institutions as well as events of national importance in his shorter fiction. R.K. Narayan prefers to select events and characters from everyday life. He presents the familiar scenes, which amuse or delight him. The most characteristic feature of his stories is his humour and gentle irony. Though the post independence Indian English short story saw a number of writers like Khuswant Singh, Bhabani Bhattacharya, Manohar Malgaonkar, Arun Joshi, Chaman Nahal and others, it is pertinent to give a brief account of the Women short story writers who in their works, focused on women's issues. Anita Desai, Kamala Markandaya, Ruth Prawar Jhabvala, Nayantara Sahgal, Shashi Deshpande, Attia Hussain, Jai Nimbkar and quite a few other women writers wrote short sorties, projecting feminist view point.

Anita Desai has written short stories with a deep understanding of human emotions. As in her novels the strain of moral questioning, of spiritual struggle, of righteous conduct is copiously woven into the basic texture of her short stories." Her approach to her characters is that of a psychologist. While her novels are psychological studies on a macro-level, all her short stories are certainly studies on a micro-level. Ruth Prawar Jhabvala was an exceptionally skilled writer dominating the scene in the 1960s and the early 1970s". Her four short story collections – *Like Bird. Like Fishes* (1963), *An experience of India* (1966), *A Stronger Climate* (1968) and *How I Became a Holy Mother* (1976) – are aesthetically distinctive but technically defective. An Inside-outsider' and an Outside-insider' at the same time, her stories present contemporary India with a convincing faithfulness comparable to any native writer's. Her stories present the theme of East-West encounter and her profound and objective understanding of the post independence Indian scene.

That Nayantara Sahgal has a fairly good pen for the shorter fiction too is made evident by her stories like *Promising Young Woman, The Golden Afternoon* and *Martand* published in reputed journals in India and abroad. As in her novels, in her stories too, she presents upper class characters in Delhi's smart society with a bit of romance. In *Martand*, for instance, the protagonist is caught between two men — her husband Naresh, who is basically cynical and Martand, who believes that there is romance in the ordinary' and it is for this reason that she is attracted towards Martand. In the end, one of them is taken away. Martand is assassinated for being too good and also, probably, for the good. Naresh mourning Martand, had found his faith in goodness again, while I, surely as I breathed, knew that everywhere within hands' reach was evil."

Attia Hussain appeared on the scene with her collection of short stories entitled *Phoenix Fled* (1953). Her stories are little vignettes, precise, loving and exquisitely true in fact and spirit." They present the feudal society of pre-independent India. To read them is as if one has drawn aside parted a curtain or opened a door, and strayed into the past.. To read them is like wrapping oneself up in ones mothers wedding sari, lifting the family jewels out of a faded box and admiring their glitter, inhaling the musky perfume of old silks in a camphor chest. Almost forgotten colours and scents."

In her stories "Tradition" and 'Customs' are acknowledged legislatures of human life. Her world is static and most people seem to be complacent in their own world. Her women characters are the most pitiable ones. She voices her protest against incompatible marriages, male dominance and women's economic exploitation.

Bharati Mukherjee hails from a traditional Bengali family. Her first collection of short stories entitled *The Middle Man and Other Stories* depicts the experience of the immigrants before and after their immigration to the USA. The protagonists in her stories are either married or divorced and they have an inclination to form relationships which end up in sexual misadventure. Kamala Das has also published quite a few short stories in Malayalam and English. Her one volume of short stories in English is *Padmavathi, the Harlot and Other Stories.* Her stories are a re-affirmation of women, women reclaimed in body and spirit. She speaks a language that challenges the male order. Her stories must be read from a Dravidian matriarch point of view. But an indication of... A Dravidian matriarch among Indian Memshabibs can be gathered from the limited usefulness other works in English.*5

Jai Nmibkar, in her *The Lotus Leaves and Other Stories,* deals with middleclass Indian life. Apart from dealing with various themes, she works her way adroitly through a complex situation to a coherent resolution. Technically the stories are tightly knit units, consciously developed into artistic wholes. She does not make use of what is conventionally called 'beginning', and her brevity skillfully skips long introductions that would have distracted the reader from the action of the story. In the words of M.K. Naik,

> Her stories deal realistically with middle class Maharastrian life, often with an acute perception of the complexity of (the) human motives.

Nergis Dalal shows her versatility by attempting various genres such as articles, middles, novels and short stories. Her short stories include a collection entitled. *The Nude* and a long short story for children named *The Birthday Present.* Dalal exploits her journalistic skills in narrating her stories which are, for this reason, branded journalistic. Her descriptions are both accurate and poetic as can be illustrated later. The scientific precision of journalism and the poetic flourishes of literature get blended in her writing. This is what makes her style unique. But she makes use of sensation or melodrama to lend her stories a touch of fascination. This is made up for as her themes are socially relevant in the present-day world. They are environment – friendly'. They condemn the harmful cultural norms and the deleterious prejudices of our civilized society. Some of her stories have received special commendation. 'The sacrifice', 'The Nude' were awarded prizes in short story competitions. 'The Exile' alone is marked out for praise by M.K. Naik. Most of the stories are set in the foot hills of the Himalayas or in small towns of the Garhwal region. Only "Once for the Asking" is an exception, being set in London. Among the major themes of the stories in this collection are: Sex, unhappy marriages, the foreigner in India, and the women writer, wild life, environment, animals etc.. Thus her short stories are not only interesting and informative but also reveal the humane side of Dalal.

'The Nude', a short story whose title the collection bears, looks - pornographic like the painting of a beautiful nude girl. In fact it mocks at the follies of a civilization which teaches to enjoy the painting of a beautiful scene and ignore the original scene in Nature. Robie De Silva paints the picture of Mrs. Oliver who has posed for him in the Nude. As a good painter, he discovers an apt model for his painting in her and as a virile man, he enjoys her beauty. The description is erotically provocative, evoking the same passion as experienced by Robie.

> Under his hand her skin was warm and glowing, gently burning and enveloping him in its warmth. She lifted one arm lazily and wrapped it about him. He was aware of nothing now but the steady beating of his own blood, and the softness, the warmth, into which he was plunging, disappearing into dark recesses which he had not known existed. (47)

Robie successfully completes the painting and it comes out marvelously well. It earns him not only a big fortune but also great fame. Mrs. Oliver receives a brochure with an imprint of the painting on it. She takes the hundred rupee note and places the brochure on the table. Then her husband arrives and she sets his food on the table. He looks at the painting and as 'he raised his eyes he caught sight of his wife, standing at the sink, her enormous waist wrapped around with a dirty apron, her head bundled in a scarf, her dress uneven and baggy'.[49) He does not know that the dame who posed in the painting is his own wife. Unlike the artist, he fails to discover the beauty in her. Instead, having seen the painting on the brochure he discovers the ugliness in his wife and is filled with revulsion.

> He felt furious and frustrated. He slammed his hand hard on the table. "Now there's a woman if you like. Something to come home to. Not a bag of old clothes like you." He glanced again at the picture and he felt the injustice sharpening, growing, persecuting him, filling him with a brooding shame for being married to a woman with fat legs and a body like a tub of lard. Blindly in his anger and frustration he left his food and slammed out of the house. Inside him was the rising urgency of sex which he would ease somewhere with some woman he had bought, or in drink (49-50).

Mrs. Oliver, knowing the ignorance and impulsive behaviour of her husband, smiles to herself secretly. This clearly shows how people fail to appreciate and enjoy the original beauty of Nature as they get conditioned by culture which dictates their aesthetic sensibility. Thus, they indulge in vicarious pleasures rather than enjoy the real ones. But the creative artist, being free from the cultural dictates, perceives this and tries to make us understand it through his work.

'The Beautiful One' is a short story about Nina. She marries Dr. Chander, a professor. The professor thinks that she will be as happy as he is. He ignores her need for love. He is always absorbed in his research on medieval history and forgets his own erotic impulses. Nina cannot bear it any longer and begins to go out with Suresh, a scholar. But the professor does not take notice of it. At last, a senior colleague warns him seriously about it and urges him to advise his wife not to see the young scholar very often. Accordingly, he conveys this to Nina calmly. She feels enraged and lashes out at him:

> I will go out with whoever I please and do exactly what I want to do. Just because I don't exist for you, doesn't mean other men don't find me desirable. You are not a man you are just a machine, dry and filled with straw instead of blood, I'm a woman, and I'm beautiful. Do you think I want to spend my life alone with neither passion nor friendship given to me? Why did you marry me? You are happy with your books and your work. You could have kept a housekeeper instead. You don't need a wife. (56)

He feels shocked and agitated; yet he gets immersed in his book as soon as he looks at it. She feels disgusted with his frigidity and leaves him forever. She elopes with Suresh and the sensation dies out as time passes.

Nina is not very happy with Suresh as he is too jealous to bear even her friendship with other men. He even starts locking her in her room. She can bear it no longer and has a bitter row about it. Then he commits suicide. She then becomes a model for a living. She lives comfortably and eventually finds the present husband. But he is also very jealous and does not allow her even to talk to men. Now she realizes her blunder in leaving the Professor. She says to her friend:

> It's a pity one doesn't realise these things until it is too late. Nothing I could have done would have disturbed Chander. He was the ideal husband for me, if only I had realised it before. (60)

Civilization and culture often pervert human nature to the extent that men forget the very purpose of human life. In such a case, being beautiful is not fun at all and becomes a source of sorrow and pain.

'The Intruder' brings out another aspect of our civilization, which divides a person into mind and body. It throws light on the disharmony caused between couple, on account of the incompatibility of their temperaments, a consequence of our civilization. Mr. Vale is a great scholar, devoted to his research. He loses his first wife who has always helped him greatly in his academic work. Then he marries a gymnasium instructor of a girls school. She ideally thinks of making him a strong man by taking him for long walks. But he detests physical exercises as much as he loves his academic work. Moreover, he starts feeling that she is an intruder, not a life-partner. She hates his bookish work and feels suffocated in the house that is against her taste. She realizes that her shoe does not and cannot fit the role expected of her in that house. Soon she begins to feel the presence of Mr. Vale's dead wife in everything in the house and to consider herself an intruder. She tries to convince her husband to change himself and their house in vain. Her failure makes her angrier and she feels as if she were told to go away:

> With sudden determination she went up and tugged furiously at the curtains. She tugged and tugged, shivering and numb with terror until at last they fell with a tearing rending sound, covering her completely. She began to struggle but the thick slippery material was everywhere. She tried to scream but something cold and fleshless closed around her throat. She felt herself sinking into a black bottomless pit. (94)

She is found dead the following morning. Thus the intruder leaves Mr. Vale by committing suicide mysteriously. The body loses the battle as our civilization prefers our mind to the body.

'Ranjit's Wife' also finds fault with the hypocrisy of our civilization Ranjit loves and marries Lila. He says that there is no other beauty for him in the world than her and she duly reciprocates his sentiment by telling him that there is no more pleasure for her in the world than to please him. She obeys him in everything to the extent that she gives up her own tastes. She wears conventional clothes and never uses any make-up according to his wishes. But he gradually loses interest in her and finds himself in love with Vanita, a young lady who is modern in her tastes. He wants to live with Vanita for ever and to divorce Lila, his wife. One day, he puts forth this proposal to his wife. She is shocked and finally requests him to give her two months. He agrees to this and leaves happily.

Lila goes to Ranjit's lawyer and learns from him that she is going to get a good amount as alimony after divorce. Then she takes Meera's help to get her hair cut short and buy cosmetics and fashionable clothes. She transforms herself into a charming young lady. She gets a new friend, Kamal Bhat through Anil, Meera's husband. The following day, she consents to go with him to a hotel. She enjoys a nice dinner and a wonderful dance with him. It so happens that Ranjit also comes to the same hotel with his love, Vanita. He sees his wife dancing with another man. He finds extraordinary beauty in her and the pangs of jealousy in himself. Now they meet for a formal introduction of one another. They leave after the party.

Kamal drops Lila at her home in his car. As she enters the house, she finds her husband there already to her surprise. But she is not scared nor apologetic as she once used to be. She coolly addresses him and asks to pour her the drink that he is having at the moment. He obeys her and she takes the drink. He can no longer contain himself and bursts out saying. "How dare you go out looking like a painted strumpet". She retorts, 'Aren't you rather forgetting that you should concentrate your reforming efforts on the new girl friend? "Sighing with relief, she adds that she is now free to do whatever she likes. Being provoked, he accusingly says, you sound as though had kept you in purdah all these years" (122) She asserts that she has indeed been kept in purdah all these ten years without being allowed to look beautiful and attractive. He says that she liked being simple. She replies that she has done so only to please him by obeying him. Thus she succeeds in making him realize his own folly. Now he comes round to her way and expresses his wish to live with her and to forget his proposal of divorce. She wants to make sure of it so she teasingly says to him:

> I'm sorry Ranjit. I don't think I want to forget about the divorce. I find it very enjoyable to do as I please, to dress as I please, to go out dancing and to find that others think I am beautiful. After all these years, it's intoxicating. I don't want to come back to you and the same dreary old routine. (123)

He then agrees to allow her being modern and fashionable. He tells her, "it need not be the same, I may have been unwise – I do find you quite intoxicating this way, Lila"(123). She does not give in immediately but she nonetheless agrees to consider his request. She will wait for two months to make sure that Ranjit is sincere. She consents to go with him the following day to a hotel. Thus she achieves her goal of winning her husband back, without getting upset.

This story, like others, deals with the relations between a wife and her husband. It shows how a man imposes cultural restraints that make his beautiful wife simple and unattractive and then runs after a modern young lady. It gives such women caught up in a crisis, the necessary confidence and courage to teach a lesson to their husbands without getting agitated. It throws light on the inner conflict within us, between our cultural norms and the novel fads and fashions of our civilization.

"One for the Asking" and *"The Red Pavilion"* share one thing in common. They illustrate the predicament of the women who love and lose. The first story is narrated by the protagonist. He is an Indian who works in a factory at Richmond in London. He is lonely. Once he meets a girl at

Regents Park Zoo. They become good friends in a few minutes. She was born to a Japanese mother and an English father. Her name is Eiko. She expresses her disillusionment about the English, perhaps because her father has betrayed her, though she never talks about it.

> You know I was brought up to believe that the English loved animals and were kind to them, but this is the most depressing zoo. I have ever visited. Those poor sad elephants, unwashed and scruffy, and those poor, listless cats in their damp cages, longing for a bit of sun. How I wish I could ship them all back to their own countries. (16)

Eiko is happy that he is from India. She accompanies him to an eating place and accepts his offer to dine with him. She eats hungrily. After dinner she goes with him to his flat and stays mere for the night. She has no possessions of her own. She stays with him till he leaves for India. She learns Indian cooking and cooks with great skill. She exhibits great dexterity in bed manners. And she keeps his home tidy. Now he is so happy with her that he often doubts if his luck is a reality or a dream. He feels that everybody wishes to have an Eiko in his life.

Two years quickly pass by and he has to leave for India. He can neither take Eiko with him nor leave her behind

> And then before I knew it, my two years were up and it was time to go home, back to India. Eiko received the news with her usual calm, but I was in a terrible state. I wanted to take her back with me, to get married and take her as my bride, but the thought of bringing this exotic flower into my orthodox family, chilled me. I could imagine the coldness with which she would be received. The questions they would ask about her background, her family. They might even want her horoscope (20).

She goes to the airport to see him off. They sit and sip coffee. He wants none to interfere with their last few precious moments when his colleague arrives and it gives him a book on India's Five Year Plans. He thanks him very formally. As he gets into the plane; he watches Eiko walk away with his colleague into the night.

In the other story, *'The Red Pavilion'*, Miss Turner is the victim. She is an elegant lady, a spinster of forty-five. She has gained respect among her neighbours. She has never allowed anybody to know her past personal life. She has been very tactful in avoiding answering the personal questions. She never accepts any invitation from anybody to any party. But none can refuse her offer. Her tea and other dishes are superb. She often goes to the club to change her library books. The people of that small hill station have not only accepted her but also liked her.

One day, Mr. Kapoor shows Miss Turner the book. *The Red Pavilion,* by W.H. Travers, and asks her whether she has read it. She just asks him if she should have read it. All the people tell her that it is all about them. She browses through book while she hears unsavoury comments about it being given to her. She is told that it is a good book. Except her, everybody is excited about it as it describes clearly the characters that are like them. Moreover, it is a best-seller and praised unanimously by critics. It is about the passionate love affair between a young Indian woman and a middle - aged Englishman. It ends unhappily as the Englishman returns inevitably to his own land.

Mrs. Peters manages to get the book autographed by the author. She is proud of it but envied for it. As she is invited to tea by Miss Turner she goes to her house. She is greatly amazed to find the signature of Miss Turner similar to the autograph in her copy of the book. Now all the mystery about Miss Turner unravels for her. She asks her about it and confirms her discovery. Then Mrs. Peters is requested to keep it secret. When she expresses her inability to do so. Miss

Turner says that she will have to leave the place if the secret about herself is out. Thus betrayed in love by the Englishman, she has to lead a lonely life.

All these stories present situations of life where men take advantage of their patriarchal privilege to enjoy themselves often to the disadvantage of the women who therefore have to suffer a great deal. However, women also have certain privileges which very few of them make use of. Sometimes we find a few women stronger than their men. The men feel suffocated in such a situation and may resort to a violent course of action. "The Alabaster Goddess" illustrates this. It reads like a detective story.

A police officer goes to a hill-station in search of peace. He is led to the temple of the Alabaster Goddess for shelter when it is about to rain heavily. It is really very comfortable there. 'To his great surprise an old monk speaks to him in good English. The monk has expected his visit and tells him about his past.

He is Harold Jerrold. A civil engineer, he was engaged in some construction work in Dehra Dun. He was reputed for being clever, scholarly and meek and so was liked by all. He married a woman notorious for her violent and unpredictable temper. Thus no servant stayed with them for long. One day he brought a Garhwali boy who was badly in need of work. The boy worked patiently, withstanding all her violence. One day he found his wife (was) shaking the boy violently holding his hair in a vicious grip, with a look of devilish pleasure on her face. He lost control over himself and shook her by the shoulder and gave her a strong push. Though very large of build and strong, she fell down, crashing into a chair. She rose and cursed them in a vile and disgusting manner. She considered him a cowardly shrimp. He just remained calm for a few days. Then, one night, he mixed two sleeping pills in her drink, which she drank without any suspicion. When she was fast asleep, he suffocated her to death with a pillow. Then he and the boy made their way to the temple to escape from the police.' They became monks and renovated the old dilapidated temple. Strangely enough, the old monk was interested in the history of the Mogul empire. He studied it assiduously and wrote a book about it. He gave it to the officer for publication and surrendered himself to him. But the officer thought and said to himself. "Who was I to disturb the peace of a man's heart, or the quiet of the hills". (43) He therefore took the manuscript and left the place without arresting him.

Dalal strikes a good balance in presenting characters and incidents without being carried away by any bias in these stories. She respects the faith and beliefs of the simple folk and mocks at the people who ridicule them. The Sacrifice's a story about Mr. Triana, a European tourist visiting India. He has seen the lush pastures the green hills, the sloping tea estates, the newly constructed dams, the ruins and temples. Now he wants to see the famine stricken areas, starved women with hanging breasts and children with rickety limbs and swollen bellies. He is accompanied by his sister and another young lady. Pritam Singh, an ex-army officer, drives his car for him.

Mr. Triana and his party stop for lunch. It is very hot. All the way, he ridicules India. He has a very poor opinion of Indian customs. He repeats it at lunch and Pritam Singh remains silent. Mr Triana feels enraged about his failure to evoke a response from Singh. So he again tries to provoke him by commenting on India:

> Floods, famine, corruption, greed and overpopulation. And there is nothing you can do about it without foreign aid. And yet you have the nerve to call yourself independent. (26)

Pritam Singh still controls himself. After lunch, they leave for the Dak Bungalow. He tells Mr. Triana that people are more interesting than the old fort as they once practised human sacrifice to the rain god. They are not allowed to do it now and they attribute the famine to this. To answer the tourists bewilderment at it, he says;

> Life is expendable here. It means one mans life to save hundreds. They would probably consider it barbarous to send men to kill each other as in war. (27)

But Mr. Triana contradicts him and supports the war. It gets dark when they reach the old fort. Drawn by the noise and the lights, a few gaunt villagers and sick children, like ghosts and skeletons moving, arrive there. The women are really shocked to see them. Mr. Triana wants to take a few pictures of them. But they want him to come to their place for this. He then says for fun that he wants to see a human sacrifice.

In his enthusiasm, Mr. Triana goes alone to their village the next day. He finds a young woman, half-naked, with her skinny baby at her naked breast. He puts his fleshy hand on her bony shoulder only to move her out of the shadow for taking a picture. But it brings the entire village there. The people move closer to him. He is shocked and tries to pacify them by offering them his money. They do not care for his money and drive their knives into him. For whatever reason it may be, it starts to rain heavily. The people are happy, celebrating it. Thus Mr. Trianas arrogance itself kills him. It is a very gripping story. Commenting on this story, Venugopal and Hegde remark. The Sacrifice", which deals with violence and superstition, with remarkable perception, is another of her successful stories.[17]

"The Temple Bells" is another story in which a robber who is skeptical of the popular faith about the temple bells is caught by the villagers of the village at the foot of the hill, on

which there is this temple. The villagers believe that the deity protects them. They contribute to the temple bells, which ring melodiously for them. They believe that the bells warn them in times of danger. Akhtar Singh is the village schoolmaster. His cousin, Dilip Singh, persuades him to join him in robbing the temple jewels. One evening, they go along with the villagers to the temple. After worshiping, the villagers leave the hill and hide behind a wall. Akhtar Singh and his cousin enter the temple. Dilip Singh breaks open the lock and enters the inner shrine. He removes the jewels and packs them safely. Akhtar Singh, who has faith in the temple bells warns his cousin. But Dilip Singh ridicules him. As they are climbing down Akhtar's legs accidentally get caught in the ropes of the bells. As he is rolls down, the bells start ringing. The villager's wakeup, go and catch them red handed. Later the police arrest them.

"The Silver Stallion" is a story of faith being rewarded. In a Rajasthani village struck by a severe famine, Jai Singh. a poor farmer, is forced to sell his live stock except Moti, their beautiful stallion. Now he has to sell even this favourite horse to buy a pump set. He and his son, Bishen, take it to the Pushkar Fair a hundred miles away. It is a big fair where thousands of animals are auctioned-Bishen is very unhappy about it. He wants to avoid selling Moti. He believes that his wish will be granted if he lights a lamp and floats it on the water in the lake.

So he does it with a wish that they would get money to buy a pump set without having to sell Moti. The sight of several lamps floating on the lake against the background of the Naghills lends immense beauty to the ful-moon night of the month of *Kartik*.

On the balcony of a tall building at Puskar, Father Kerry tells Rajendra Singh he has a scheme for making the Rajasthani villages green. Rajendra Singh agrees to grant him the amount for the purpose. Then they suddenly see the stallion and wonder:

> From the darkness where the hills cast their blue shadow, a horse erupted into the light. The horses mane and tail were silvered by the moon and streamed out behind. Against the thunder of his hooves the air rushed past. His legs moved with grace and precision and it was like watching the effortless flight of a bird, so smooth and swift was his passage. Only as an afterthought did they see the small figure flattened on me horses' back.(83)

Rajendra Singh at once decides to buy that horse. He and Father Kerry search for it and find it. Bishen is asked whether he will sell it. He replies that he will sell it to the highest bidder. But they notice his sorrow about losing Moti. Then they learn the conditions under which he is forced to sell it They sympathize with, him. Father Kerry now tells his friend that he will start his programme with Bishen's village. He then tells Bishen that he can have the pump set without selling Moti. He asks him to inform his father about this. Bishen feels very happy and runs to his father to convey the good news. Jai Singh cannot believe his ears and comes to meet them at once. He is told that they will install a tube well in his land and that he can pay his debt when he has a good harvest. Bishen attributes this good luck to his floating of the lamp in the lake in front of the temple of the Brahma. They remember the old legend and laugh as the boy goes away happily with his stallion.

Dalal commends the innocent faith but condemns the faith of the elite in fake saints. The stories discussed before exemplify the former, while "Roses, Roses, All the Way..." illustrate the latter. The narrator has a beautiful garden. A around her house in which she grows roses. Once a stranger comes to the narrator dressed in a white sari and introduces her self as Miss Malik. Miss Malik very politely asks her for some roses. The landlady obliges her and offers her tea.

Suddenly to the consternation of the narrator Miss Malik bursts into sobs. However she calms down after some time. She then narrates her story.

Miss Malik is a wealthy spinster. She looked after her sick old mother with such devotion that she never thought of her marriage. When her mother died leaving a good fortune to her, it was too late for her to get married. She then did not know what to do. On the advice other friends she began to travel without any aim. She always felt lonely. Nobody took any genuine interest in her. She wondered if she would forever remain a solitary soul. Finally she came to that small hill station to spend the summer and found a haven in the ashram there. She has been austere since then. She used to drink several cups of tea every day. She has not drunk a drop of tea since she was told by the Swamiji not drink tea. Now it is the tea of the hostess that reminds her of those days and makes her nostalgic about her luxurious past.

The hostess asks her whether the Swamiji is equally austere. Miss Malik answers her in the affirmative. After tea, she takes a lot of beautiful roses and leaves for the ashram, accompanied by this narrator. She arranges the flowers beautifully. Then the Swamiji arrives and there is perfect silence. A bevy of girls in white are in his service. "The whole show seemed to have been exceptionally well stage – managed".(75) He begins the prayers. After the prayers, each devotee goes to him and prostrates in front of him. He offers them each a few petals, a pinch of ash and a small piece of coconut kernel. Miss Malik also has his darshan when the Swamiji goes in, she takes the narrator around the ashram. She is greatly shocked to find the Swamiji drinking an expensive brand of tea in his chamber. The shock at once causes disillusionment. She takes her baggage and stealthily leaves with her hostess for the hotel immediately. She gives up all her austerity. She orders for both a sumptuous lunch.

She goes to her room, bathes, wears a dark blue silk sari, a string of pearls, good make-up and perfume and emerges like a nymph. She is really beautiful, elegant and confident. She looks at the ashram and says to her hostess, "In fact, you might say, it is going to be roses, roses, all the way for me. (78)

"Christmas Means Love" is a fine story, depicting the tender feelings of a boy waiting for his father who has béen away for a long time and also the agony that his mother has felt in her heart trying to answer her son's questions' about his father. Arun is a six year old boy; he loves his mother very much. Yet he needs his father whom he identifies with. He is very unhappy without his father who has been away on a long tour. He waits for him desperately. His mother tells him that he will come soon. She does not know when he will come, but she expects him soon. She cleans up and decorates the house. She cooks several delicious dishes. Now Christmas is fast approaching. She starts writing a letter when she receives a telegram that he is coming on the Eve of Christmas. She feels elated and tells Arun about his fathers arrival. He goes to school very happily and tells everybody about his father's coming for Christmas. This is a pleasant surprise to his teacher.

Arun waits anxiously for his father on the Eve of Christmas. He runs out as soon as he hears the sound of a car. The car stops, his father comes out and lifts Arun with great affection. Now his mother also joins them:

> Now at last she moved stiffly to meet them, the tall man and the little boy, so absurdly alike. They saw her and the man put out his free hand and caught her to his heart. It was not a time for words but Arun asked suddenly, '"You will go away again, will you?" and a shadow crossed the radiant face. The man held them both close. No," he said slowly "never again" and turning the three of them entered the house, filled with the wonderful smells of Christmas - filled with the wonderful warmth of love. (68)

Yet another story about children is "Happiness Is a Box of Fudge" Two girls, aged twelve and fourteen are forced by their mother to allow an old man to caress them and to read to him the newspaper every day. They resent it but cannot avoid it. They don't get time for their games and fun. Yet they like eating the little piece of vanilla fudge given by the old man after reading the paper. One day they come home after school and learn that the old man had died of heart attack. Their mother takes flowers and goes to his funeral. The girls feel very happy as now they are free of the old man. The next day, the girls get a box of vanilla fugde from the daughters of the old man. They are happy that the old mans daughters too had understood their fondness for vanilla fudge.

Dalal condones stealing if it exhibits aesthetic taste. It is for her as natural as and probably nobler than the gathering of food by primitive human beings like animals in prehistoric times when there was no private property. "The Connoisseur" illustrates this. Miss Krishna is an old spinster. Her mother loved her younger sister who left her after getting married. Yet Miss Krishna served her mother till the end. She was left with a small house and a meagre income. But she had a great fascination for beautiful things, which she could ill afford. She says:

> All my life I have been starved of beautiful things. My early life was one continuous struggle. Poverty is so ugly. All those thick coarse sheets on the beds, uncarpeted floors, pottery cups and plates and ugly discarded furniture. How ones soul craves for beautiful things! (151)

She picks up whatever looks beautiful to her wherever she finds it. She is in the habit of stealthily putting it in her handbag and taking if to her house. Nobody discovers this until after she is dead. She likes the narrator who appreciates her aesthetic sense. She therefore wills all her property to her. When her sister informs the narrator of the will, she politely refuses to take the property. She sees Miss Krishna's collection and knows that they are all stolen, She finds her own clock among them. So she requests her sister to allow her to take the clock by which she can remember Miss Krishna.

"The Exiles" unravels the myth of homeland and shows how we develop an attachment to an alien land in course of time. This story has received great applause. For example, Venugopal and Hegde say: However, in an array of formula stories it is heartening when one surprisingly comes across such a true piece of art like" The Exiles" (217) It is about an English couple who have lived in India for twenty five years. Mr. Alan Wain has worked in a firm for twenty five years and has just retired. A felicitation function is arranged in his honour and is concluded with his speech expressing his gratitude to all the people who have cooperated with him all these days. They all disperse and Mr. And Mrs. Wain and their servants are busy packing the luggage. Mrs. Wain finds it hard to select things for packing. She is excited and happy about going to her homeland. When asked how she will manage there without servants and other facilities that she has enjoyed here. She smiles and says:

> I shall really enjoy the climate and I like to do my own work. It is not the same as this you know. Everything there is quite different. There is so little dust for one thing, and all the fruit and vegetables come cleaned and packaged. I shall manage very well I expect (99-100)

She does not like Indian manners and things. She feels disgusted about them. But as the days of their departure draw near, all her feelings get reversed. A strange nostalgia for Indian, and things seizes her. She now wonders why she detested them; and how it was that she could not bring herself to like them:

> Mrs. Wain looked with affection at the marigold which she would perhaps see for the last time - flamboyantly yellow or

> orange, they now seemed to her a symbol of the colour and gaiety of this country. How could she ever have disliked them? She touched one curved petal with her finger and it was soft and velvety to the touch. (106-107)

Dalal has a great concern for environmental protection. Some of her literary writings profusely exemplify this. Her descriptions of trees, animals and nature reflect this. "A Taste of Blood" is a good example of her concern for wild life. It is usual that women care for nature while men care for civilization. This story revolves round a family of a mother, son and father. The father takes his son to the forest for hunting, but the mother does not approve of this. But the father supports his sons interest in hunting. He argues with his wife about it when she objects to it:

> 'Now shut up', he said evenly. "I don't want my son to grow up a namby-pamby. I've told you before. I won't have him tied to your apron strings. I want him to be a real boy. You stop scolding him. He did a fine job with that bird. I'm proud of him." (8)

He invites his wife to go with them for fun. She is deeply hurt and is greatly worried about her son and the healthy growth of his personality. She argues with her husband against teaching him the cruel game:

> You are corrupting my child, teaching him the taste of blood. It is a corruption worse than that of sex more perverse than any perversion.(11)

He was not convinced and proudly said, '"My son is going to grow into a man". Now she wants to see if she has a chance to show his son how cruel it is to hunt dumb creatures. So she consents to go with them. They all go to the forest. The boy stays with his mother while his father goes to the lake to see if there are any ducks. After a while, a pretty little deer comes, hardly two hundred yards away from them. She feels very happy to see it and tries to share her joy with her son who is ready to shoot it with his gun. She cries aloud to him not to shoot it and the deer runs away. She sees the reeds move slowly and tells her son that there is another deer. Without waiting, he shoots at it and runs to see his prey. He screams loudly to see his father lying dead. He sobs and his mother tries to console him. The irony is that the father himself is hunted by his son and all because he had learnt the cruel game of hunting from the father.

The Nude consists of the sixteen stories discussed above. In addition to these, Dalal wrote a long story for children. It is *The Birthday Present* . It is about the preservation of animal life. It is about a dog which turns dangerous on account of the cruel treatment by a wealthy man and which resumes all its nice qualities after being looked after with love and care by a boy who received it as a birthday present. Children love to read this story and learn about the harmless and beneficent behaviour of mute animals. However, a detailed critical study of *The Birthday Present* is given separately as an extraordinary children's classic.

Nergis Dalal is accused of indulgence in sensationalism and journalese in her short stories by some critics, like Venugopal and Hegde. She has written articles and middles for papers for many years and has contributed some of the best middles which have earned her a good reputation. However, one should think the journalistic style has given her stories a new flavour. Moreover her experience with journalism lends her fiction a full-blooded realism. And not all the stories indulge in sensationalisation. Sometimes the themes demand sensationalism. "The Nude" or "Ranjit's Wife" illustrate the follies of our civilization which make us blind to real beauty. "The Beautiful One presents a professor who loves his studies and who ignores his beautiful wife who elopes with a young scholar. 'The Alabaster Goddess' shows how a woman behaves so cruelly that her meek husband has to kill her. "The Sacrifice" and "The Temple bells" relate how arrogant people who ridicule the faith of innocents cause their own downfall. "Roses, Roses, All the way 'exposes a fake saint and mocks at the auster:ties that try to oppress life itself. "A Taste of Blood" and *The Birthday Present* are about the preservation of wild life.

The writer maintains a nice balance between her different themes, which are socially relevant. Her language is lucid, graphic and often borders on the poetic. The following passage may be taken as an example of this:

> The wind sprang up with a violence that tore the leaves from the trees and tossed the branches high in the air. The clear blue hills, so sharply etched against the sky, were now shrouded in a thick gray mist, and the sky itself turned dark and menacing. (33)

To conclude, we may say that the stories of Mrs. Dalal have an amazing diversity of themes and techniques. Her major preoccupations are sex, married life, spirituality and the foreigner in India. These together with women with strong personalies figure significantly in the stories. As in the novels, the action is confined mostly to the Garhwal region of the foothills of the Himalayas". The Nude" and 'The Sacrifice' stand out among the stories as her best. The other stories too illustrate Mrs. Dalal's general concerns, which receive a fuller treatment in the novels.

REFERENCES

1. Ed. Dorothy Blair Shmer, Short Story *"The Mentor Book of Modern Asian Literature,* Tororto: The new American Library, 1969 p,321.
2. W.H. Hudson, *An Introduction :o the Study of Literature,* London: George G.harrap and Company, 1910, p. 337.
3. *Ibid.,* p. 340.
4. Ed. A. N. Dwivedi, Contempcrary Indian English Short story NOTIES *"Studies in Contempo:ary Indian English Short Stories,* New Delhi B.R.Publications, 1991, p. 10.

5. Hudson, p. 342.
6. A.N. Dwivedi, p. 9
7. C.V.Venugopal, The Indian Short Story in English, Bareilly: Prakash Book Depot, 1975, p. 2.
8. *Ibid., p.* 13.
9. M.K. Naik, p. 109.
10. K.R. Srinivasayengar, p. 182.
11. S.D. Sharma, 'Anita Desai' Ed. A.N. Dwivedi, *Studies in Contemporary Short Story,* Delhi: B.R. Publishing Corporation, 1991, p. 25.
12. John Connell, Introduction to *Phoenix Fled,* p. IX.
13. R.S. Pathak, "Attia Husain and Women Question" in Veena Noble Das (ed.), *Feminism and Literature,* New Delhi: Prestige Books, 1994, p. 133.
14. Ahmed Ali, Introduction to *Twilight,* New Delhi: Oxford University Press, 1966, p. 8.
15. Elias Mohammad, "The Short Stories of Kamala Das," *Changing Traditions in Indian English Literature.*
16. M.K. Naik, p. 253.
17. Venugopal and Hegde, p. 217.

5

The Birthday Present

AN EXTRAORDINARY CHILDREN'S CLASSIC

David Copperfield's acuteness of touch and smell, as he looks into the blank of my infancy' and recalls his earliest impressions of home, comes before us as a classic example of the portrayal of states of childhood. In this category, we may include Jane Eyre's resistance against older oppressors, Stephen Daedalus's recollecting of first memories in *The Portrait of an Artist as a Young Man;* Henry James's fresh resilient Maisie, who thrives against all odds, among adult deceit and selfishness, Paul Morel's emergent awareness of the battle lines drawn between his mother and father, Maggie Tulliver's intense experiences of childhood joys and pains. Though these works may not have been addressed to children, their art is characterized by a respect for the child's existence, and for what Dickens termed in *Hard Times* as the dreams of childhood — its airy fables; its graceful, humane, impossible adornments of the world beyond'. Furthermore the art of these writers, and the quality- of their concern for children have a powerful influence on me best among writers who have written exclusively, or especially for children in the 19th and the 20th centuries. There are now a considerable number of high quality books in the genre. In the words of Bernard T. Harrison:

> Children's literature— in particular, children's fiction — has come of age' in our times, as a distinct branch of literature's great tree.[1]

Writers of children's fiction have sought to enhance the status of children's fiction. They have emphasized that children's literature should, like all literature, offer enjoyment. But enjoyment of the best is, they claim, no easy pleasure, it ought to involve a stretching of imagination, a deepening of experience, and a heightening of awareness. According to Edgar Friedenberg,

> The writer's task lies in the respectful and affectionate nurturing of the young, and the cultivation in them of a disciplined and informed mind and heart.[2]

By way of contrast Joen Aiken, while acknowledging the educative moral powers of a well-told tale, has dwelled on the liberating, subversive qualities that a good children's book and a healthy child reader should have in common. They can see through the adult with some moral axe to grind almost before he opens his mouth — the smaller the child, the sharper the instinct,"[3] Joen Aiken who acknowledges Blake, Dickens and Charlotte Bronte, among the main influences on her own ample production of fiction written for children, provides us here with a useful clue to an appropriate critical approach to children's books, which we might link with a view of the innocent as being in itself a mode of insight.

Lewis Carroll's *Alice's Adventures in Wonderland* (1865) is an early classic written especially for children R.L. Green rightly observes on this classic thus;

> The directness of such a work was a revolution in its sphere. It was the coming to the surface, powerfully and permanently, for the first unapologetic, undocumented appearance in print for readers who rarely needed it, of liberty of thought in children's books.[4]

Geoffrey Trease, writer on literature for children, lays down the following specifications for any children's writer. According to him:

> The work must be a genuine book at all levels. When he is choosing his theme and doing his research his standards can be as adult, indeed as academic, as he likes. When he is writing then he must let the child in himself dictate much of the form. He should be a children's writer because he still retains in himself, perhaps more vividly than the average adult, the vestigial child he once was.[5]

Output of animal stories has also continued to be prolific, with horses, dogs and foxes as clear favorites. Animal stories have taken more unusual directions in such works as Richard Adams' neo-Darvinian fantasy of survival singles among rabbits in *Watership Down* (1972); or Jan Needle's *Wild Wood* (1981), which transposes *The Wind in the Willows* into an amusing socialist satire aimed at the idle-rich Edwardian bank dwellers; or the strange, disturbing tale of clockwork toys in Russell Hoban's *The Mouse and his Child* (1969). These books have attracted justifiably a good deal of attention from adults as well as from children.

Fantasy is, of course, the root and stem of much of children's fiction. In Carroll's *Alice* the many opportunities to enjoy the fantasist's escape are presented in clear tension with the actual experiences and constraints of a child's real world. In short, the fantasizing spirit is never given complete licence to evade confrontation with real events. Carroll recognized that. Without such a disciplining tension there is a danger that fantasy might feed parasitically on the shore of the imagination, weakening its capacity to give shape to actual experience. In the realm of children's books, works of fantasy since 1950 proliferated both in the West and the East.

Philippa Pearce writes mainly for younger children, say, up to twelve years. Compared with story-makers like William

Mayne or Russell Hoban, the output of Philippa Pearce has been modest. Her *A Dog So Small* (1962) is a typical piece of children's writing. In the composing of the work, she declared that

> From the very beginning — perhaps even before you think of writing a story at all – the story must grow. The idea of a story is a seed, and it grows with the slowness of natural growth.[6]

Nergis Dalal loves children and animals and writes about animals for the sake of children. 'The Birthday Present' is one such story, which had won her an award, and perhaps it is this story more than any other writings that compels affection for Dalal as a writer.

The Birthday Present[7] an extraordinary Children's Classic is a long short story published originally in 1972 by Orient Longman, and issued in 1997 by the same publishers as a Gul Mohar book. It is a story, rather a long story, meant for children (Children of all ages from six to sixty[1] as Mulk Raj Anand might have put it). It could have been conveniently subsumed under the chapter devoted to Nergis Dalal's short stories but, considering its intrinsic importance and enormous significance as a memorable children's story, is given a separate chapter and its justification should be clear by the time one has come to the end of it.

One can be passionately fond of one's dog and this passionate fondness can be infectious. This is a truism which is powerfully illustrated by Dalal's *The Birthday Present* (which, in remote way, is reminiscent of an essay that Mulk Raj Anand wrote for *The Indian Express* some years ago when his pet dog died - that was a touching elegy on the death of his dog). If a critic can lay claim to a little measure of frivolousness or playful impertinence, he might wonder and say that it is rather difficult to Judge whether Dalal's insight into canine psychology is not deeper and more unerring than that into its human counterpart.

The Birthday Present centers on the theme of dogs which are capable either of infinite love and loyalty or of boundless ferocity and violence – depending, of course, on how they are treated, with love or hate.

Dev, a little lad of ten, waits for years to acquire a beautiful pup as a birthday present from his parents. Mr. and Mrs. Malik, and when the momentous day arrives he is forced to choose between this pup and an ugly looking dog peevish and ferocious because of the ill-treatment that he has received from his master. When Dev hears the story of this dog. Rajah, from the Nawab (the original master) he (Dev) chooses to have Rajah instead of that lovely pup so that he can take good care of him and convert him into a lovable and faithful friend. The parents are initially unwilling but then they yield and Rajah is taken home from the Zemindar who has ill-treated him.

Dev, who is determined to treat Rajah compassionately, gives him medical treatment and good food quite regularly, thanks to the help he receives from that inveterate lover of dogs, the Nawab, as well as his parents who treat the whole situation with pity and understanding.

The results are bewildering. Once Rajah is his normal self, he becomes again a source of delight to all around. The description of the scene of Dev and Rajah playing together offers the reader a delightful spectacle:

> Dev began to run and Rajah ran beside him, tongue hanging out, tail wagging joyously, leaping up from time to time. Suddenly he raced ahead, ears flat on his head, tail down, running so fast that he was no more than a blur. He turned and came back, circled and flew on, running so swiftly that Dev could not keep up with him at all. Round and round he

> went, his circles narrowing around the boy, until at last he came and stood beside him, panting, his fur ruffled, his eyes shining with pleasure. He licked Dev's hand and rolled over on his back. He lay there, his mouth open as though he were laughing, asking the boy to play with him. Dev was astonished and delighted. He rolled over the grass beside Rajah, and the boy and the dog wrestled together. Rajah letting out ferocious-sounding growls from time to time, but wagging his tail hard without stopping. At last, exhausted, they sat up together, Dev with his hand on Rajahs head, and thus it was that the Nawab found them (pp. 60-61).

One is compelled to agree with Dev when he can scarcely conceal his admiration for this canine friend: You are a wonderful dog. The cleverest dog in the world" (p. 60). The Nawab adds his praise for his former ward thus: "I told you he was the best dog I ever trained" (p. 60).

Rajah proves himself to be an utterly faithful friend to Dev and his family and wins the appreciation of even the police by catching a burglar and is instrumental in the arrest of some notorious thieves. The Police Officer says thus: "Thanks to your son and his dog. We have caught a really nasty bunch of thieves. I really think they both deserve medals." The story concludes - and rightly too with the following words of the Nawab which could be used to express the quintessence of Dalal's thematic preoccupation in this story:

> In the beginning I was afraid that you would never succeed with Rajah. He was so savage and so full of hatred. But now you have got a wonderful dog and you deserve him. It needed courage to take a starved wild animal and turn him, with kindness and love and lots of patience, into this beautiful, faithful animal. But for you, Rajah would have been lying in a cold damp grave."(p. 86).

Dalal's observation of the canine world and canine psychology is astonishingly keen. In support of this statement we could give several instances. When total rapport has been established between Rajah and "his little master Dev (p.65),

Rajah refuses the food that is offered to him by Mrs. Malik, Dev's mother. He would not just relish food in his master's absence. Further, Dalal knows that intimacy between man and dog is possible only with the passage of time. It cannot be instantaneous. Like men watching dogs, dogs too must watch men before they can put trust in them.

Let's have a close look at the following passage:

> The Nawab leaned over and picked up one of the small creatures. It opened its wide pink mouth and gave a tiny bark. Dev laughed. The puppy was so small it fitted easily into the palm of his hand and yet it barked (p. 4).

Only one who has lived with dogs for long can give such intimate, accurate and evocative pictures. The same comment holds good in the case of the following snatch of the Nawab's conversation:

> Come along. Your puppy is waiting for you. He is *a fine strong little fellow.* Next year you can show him in the puppy-class at the dog show. *He has his mother's sweet temper, his father's good looks. Look* after him well'(Emphasis added) (p.7)

Dalal's description is so sensitively done that one wonders whether she is dealing with canine kids or their human counterparts.

When Dev sees the miserable condition that Rajah has been reduced to by the Zemindar, he asks: What kind of man would do such a thing to a dog? 'This question is so vital that it assumes a significance, which transcends the context and becomes universal. In other words, we know it is not merely Dev's question and the anguished cry of the author.

And Dev's affectionate treatment of the ailing dog is equally touching:

> The garage was large and roomy and at the back were a few empty packing cases. Dev pushed and pulled these about to make a small secluded place for the dog, where he would feel

> safe. He spread the blanket down and Rajah settled himself down wearily. Dev crouched beside him and gently removed me muzzle. Rajah did not even lift his head. Dev had a hard time keeping back the tears when he looked at him. Every rib was visible and the hair harsh and patchy. He was covered with sores and wounds. Gently, Dev took the ointment the Nawab had given him and spread it wherever he could. Rajah did not move. (p. 37)

One feels that Dalal's portrait of Rajah must have come from the life. Rajah's recovery is not shown to be quick or instantaneous but slow and steady. That is how Dalal makes everything in *The Birthday Present* credible.

The Nawab who appears to be the mouthpiece of Dalal says: 'A well-trained, well-adjusted dog will disobey or attack only under extreme provocation, Dogs respond to kindness even more than human beings do."(p. 54)

A close reading of the text reveals that Dalal has wielded her language extremely sensitively. That is evident not only in the names that she gives to her dogs and bitches (Rajah and Golden Sheba, for instance) but the metaphors she uses too. (The use of the phrase 'fur ball' for a pup is a case in point)

The entire philosophy of Dalal in relation to dogs is summed up by the Nawab when he says: "And in the whole world you can have no lover friend than a dog".

The Birthday Present is easily a model specimen of children's literature. If critics choose to ignore this work it would be positively unwise because it is a tour de force of Dalal in the short story genre. In fact, it makes such absorbing reading that one wonders if it is a story of dogs or humans. What needs to be taken note of in particular is the way Dalal is all along careful to make her writing sound utterly natural, un forced – nay, even admirable.

If any one is tempted to praise this work in superlative terms he needs our indulgence. In fact, *The Birthday Present* not only deserves an award but it deserves to be re-issued as a children's classic by the Children's Book Trust of India, and its copies made available at a price well within the reach of our children all through the country.

REFERENCES

1. Bernard T. Harrison. "Literature for Children: A Radical Genre in Borisford (ed.), *The Present*, London: Penguin Books, 1983.
2. See Standards of "Criticism for Childrens Literature," ed. N. Chambers (ed.), *The Signal Approach to Children's Books*, Harmondsworth, 1980.
3. See The Author as the Ally of the Reader,' eds. M.Meek et al. in *The Cool Web*. 1974.
4. Quoted in Green, R.L. *Tellers of Tales: Children and their Books from 1800 to 1964*, 1965.
5. See The Historical Novelist at Work, in G.Fox (ed.), *Writers, Critics and Children*. 1976.
6. See *Writing a Book*, ed. M. Meek
7. Nergis Dalal, *The Birthday Present*, New Delhi: Orient Longman, 1972.
8. Reported by G.S. Balarama Gupta in his book, *Mulk Raj Anand*, JIWE Publishers, Gulbarga.

6

Nergis Dalal's Middles and Other Journalistic Writings

NEVER A DALAL MOVEMENT

Nergis Dalal the novelist and short story writer is also a distinguished journalist. As a distinguished journalist, she has been contributing to the leading newspapers and magazines both in India and abroad. She has written 'Middles', a genre of journalistic literature and thousands of her middles on various subjects and issues have appeared in leading newspapers, like *The Times of India, The Statesman, Pioneer* and *The Indian Express.* Khushwant Singh, a former editor of the *Illustrated Weekly of India,* aptly says, "Nergis Dalal's Middles will be appetiser before the substantial repast, provided by her splendid little novel *Minari*".[1] It is said 'A middle' is more than a space filler in a newspaper; it has become a distinct literary form. And since it is usually given the pride of place in the center of an editorial page it is much the most widely read column of any paper. Both the editor and the reader expect a lot from the middle' writer; compactness restricted to a single theme, conciseness to a point of constriction (not one spare word); lightness - the narrative interspersed with anecdotes, wit and levity - and then a moral in the form of a punch line at the end'[2].

Shatish Aikant's observation on the Middles is interesting:

> We are living in an age when culture, to a large extent, is shaped by media centrality. However, despite the burgeoning electronic media, the printed word has neither lost its power nor its relevance. And hence Newspaper, an important vehicle of cultural literacy, will continue to exercise its influence in the daily lives of people, touching the areas of both high culture and popular culture. For an enlightened and reflective reader it is the editorial page that provides him the food for thought. A 'Middle' occupies literally the middle space on this page, and usually catches the quick attention of the reader. It appeals to him because of its style, neither highbrow nor pedestrian, and yet it conveys enough substance to delight and to inform. It is this characteristic quality of a middle that draws readership as diverse as there are topics dealt with by their writers. Their sallies are enriched with varied experiences, and it is not only the established writers who take to it, but many others; professionals, civil servants, even housewives, if they have a flair for writing. It is this variety that makes the reading such a delightful fare. The reader is all the wiser by knowing little known facts, viewpoints and vignettes. Very often a Middle' can function as a subaltern discourse, subverting the conventional hierarehical representations, particularly of political and social life.[3]

In his preface to *A Medley of Middles* another famous well known writer K.V. Chacko observes thus:

> The lighter vein has always been a favorite branch of creative writing in the English speaking world. Down to earth humour, socio - political satire, spoofing at fads and snobberies, and intellectually stimulating wordplay are some of the manifestations of the lighter vein muse. The English language, maybe due to its pliability, is a better medium for the light muse than most Indian languages.

The 'Middle' has become today the most sought-after branch of lighter vein writing. Amidst the drab and nauseating political and economic pontificators we find in the editorial pages of most newspapers, the middle stands out as a source of relief and entertainment. The popularity of the middle is catching up and even the mofussil and regional English dailies have started to publish middles. There was a time when ones creative abilities were recognised only if one had made it to the middle columns of *The Times of India.* Today many other papers - *The Indian Express, The Hindustan Times, National Herald, Hitawada, Nagpur Times,* for example - give us one daily middle. There is an esoteric tribe of middle writers scattered throughout the country.

> I am happy to note that over the years I have been fortunate to have secured a little niche in this enchanted land by being able to publish over 150 middles and lighter vein pieces in various journals. But I do not forget here the traumas—if a middle writer aspiring to appear" in the national dailies. The national papers and magazines appear to be still cherishing the colonial myth that English creativity is an exclusive preserve of the metropollinate pen-pushers. Of late there is a slight improvement in the situation as we are reading middles and other creative works by (the) "Mofussil writers in the big-big" journals. Bombay intellectual imperialism is coming to a close.[4]

Khushwant Singh speaks of the quality of middles, and says that of all the Indian national newspapers, *The Times of India* excels in the quality of its middles. And of all the middle - writers no one is rated higher than *ARIES. ARIES* was also asked to write for *The Indian Express.* In the last 30 years over thousand Aries middles have been written and over 300 and above have been published.

The fascinating thing about Nergis Dalal is that she wrote and published her middles under the pseudonym ARIES. Why did she chose such a pseudonym? Nergis Dalal herself explains, I can't remember now why I chose ARIES as a pseudonym. It seems to have bothered a lot of people being a male sign. It is difficult to explain why I write under a pseudonym at all, except that initially. I enjoyed the feeling of anonymity it gave me. The last thing I expected was for ARIES to become well known, and Nergis Dalal to remain completely obscure.

Khushwant Singh met Nergis Dalal in person. It was a very pleasant surprise to discover that ARIES was not a man but a woman - and an extraordinarily attractive woman at that, sophisticated, urbane, soft spoken and erudite. While responding to his question why she was not writing something more ambitious than middles she handed over to him her first novel *Minari,* bearing for the first time her real name. She also said:

> I enjoy writing middles; and have -written at some time or the other, of practically everything that ever happened to me. On the whole they are meant to be light-hearted, gay and amusing. Letters, often objecting strongly, and even violently, to what I have written, came as something of a surprise. But there are nicer letters too-from Peter Herring in Denmark, offering me a case of his wonderful liquor and inviting me to be his guest if I ever visited Denmark – from an entire officers Mess in Ladakh, telling me the first thing they looked for in The Times was an *ARIES* middle - and best of all, from the other middle writers saying how much they had enjoyed a particular middle."[6]

Nergis Dalal does not think that writing middles' is an easy task. "However", she states, nevertheless writing middles is still one of my favourite occupations. I have through the years become familiar with other authors of *'middles'*—and since they write inevitably about themselves. I could now compile a fairly extensive dossier on each of the 'regulars.' I know a great deal about their families, and their likes and dislikes"[7]. Dalal is of the view that a woman writer writes middles' in a better way than men writers.

Nergis Dalal's middles are not loosely-knit articles. Middle; according to Fowler's dictionary is a short-essay usually of some literary value on some subject of a permanent and general interest rather than of a topical and political interest.

Dalal's middles have their own 'compactness, lightness and punch. The middles in *Never a Dull Moment* reflect really the remarkable versatility, of the author and her uncanny talent' for deriving entertainment from the most ordinary subjects of human life.

A selection of sixty middles written by Nergis Dalal was published by Orient Longman under the title *Never a Dull Moment.*[8] which happens to be the title of the first middle that reflects the theme and outlook, (looking at the silver linings of the dark cloud of life as does the author) running through most of the middles. The writer first shows us the dark cloud and then gradually and convincingly leads us to perceive the silver lining. Her ironic vision brings out the humour of the various situations of life, which are otherwise unperceivable. Her humaneness endows her articles with fine sentiments. Her facility with the language makes her expression lucid and her humour effective. All these features are found in other writings as well, such as her innumerable articles published in newspapers and journals from time to time and her novels and short stories. She is unconventional and moderate in her views. She is free from dogmas, either revolutionary or reactionary. In her writings, she is committed to the larger good of humanity. This commitment enables her to look at the negative side of a situation or an individual with compassionate understanding and tolerance. A comprehensive, but brief survey of her middles and articles would bring out the truth of these claims.

In her *"Never a Dull Moment"*, Nergis Dalal gives out that she lives with her family on the first floor of a house where the ground floor is occupied by a Technical Institution. Therefore, their apartment is mistaken for different public places by different people. For example, the students preparing for examinations mistake it for a library and enter it to read books. Similarly, a group of people come in the morning and go upstairs to make a few phone calls, mistaking it for an office. When they are told it is a private phone, they are greatly surprised and rush out, apologizing profusely. In this way, the writer is constantly disturbed. This is indeed, a great inconvenience to her; yet, she learns to take pleasure in it. She, therefore, says: Still there is one advantage, we never have a dull moment. Anything can happen, and does!'. This and a few other middles bring out the positive aspect even of a place of disadvantage.

Dalal has not got a house of her own and her friend whom she visits remarks that it is very dreadful of her not to have a house. She looks around at the beautiful garden of her friend and appreciates it. Yet she does not regret it and remembers the lovely flower garden that she has grown. Now she feels happier than her friend as she relishes the pleasant memories of all the houses that she has lived in. She writes in "The Heart Remembers."

> But having no roots anywhere has compensations. We have memories of all the places we have stayed in, and the memories are never unpleasant, for the heart has a way of rejecting all that is not beautiful and storing only that which is lovely and good.[9]

Similarly, in "The Breeding Shahin", she shows how anticipation is more exciting than realization, by describing how people vainly endeavour to see a breeding Shahin (p. 15-16).

Most of the middles deal with people. They humorously but sympathetically depict the weaknesses of (the) people and then highlight their merit that effectively prevails onus to condone their weaknesses. These middles are relished for their perfect blend of humour and humanity. "The Bachelor Friend" is a good example. Dalal's bachelor friend drops in frequently and asks for several cups of coffee. He, sometimes, stays for dinner. She, often feels so annoyed that she thinks that it is an excellent idea "to tax bachelors at a higher rate than married men. "But, one day, he invites her for dinner, calling it "an informal little affair." This is a great surprise to her. When she arrives she has many misconceptions about his hospitality and the tidiness of his apartment. But the treat is so excellent and his apartment is so unexpectedly tidy that she amends her opinion and infers: "I can only surmise that the Finance Minister has also been entertained fairly recently by a bachelor and has amended his tax proposals accordingly-for once I am in wholehearted agreement with him."

Dalal does not hesitate, in some of her middles, to deflate a person who exhibits vanity. "Mario and the Indian girls," illustrates this. Mario is a Swiss young man, travelling around the world. He earns a little money by sending" photographic essays" to Swiss papers. So the writer suggests that he take pictures of the marble sculptures of the local temple. But he says that his people are interested in people, rather than in dead marble things. So, one evening, he visits the club where he intends to meet some Indian girls. To his chagrin, all the ladies gathered in a corner of the club and remained aloof. Thus his lively interest in Indian girls is not reciprocated. So he comments: "They are pretty and graceful but high." She cannot understand what he means by the word high." Of course he later clarifies himself by saying that they are 'Not friendly at all'. [11]

Dalal often refuses to conform to the accepted norms and it usually results in a good outcome. Once she takes a correspondence course in journalism. Her instructor never approves of her responses in the assignments because she never follows the instructions in them. Consequently, their lessons become a series of acrimonious arguments and discussions. The short story which he disapproves strongly wins her the first prize. Similarly, she never bothers about how a middle is expected to be written. Yet she is always successful in writing middles and she has earned a good name for them (pp.19-20). She makes fun of the conventional ways of learning languages. She depicts how a language-learning situation sometimes brings great fun;

> One of the linguaphone records consists of nothing but sounds. The first time this was played, the dog rushed out, barking

> and growling, obviously under the impression that another particularly ferocious and aggressive dog had got in.[12]

She laughs at the language manuals for giving a stock of artificial phrases. "The pen of my aunt-illustrates this. She, however, adds. It would, I suppose, have an eerie charm all its own".[13]

Dalal does not seem to entertain feminist ideas. She honestly admits her feminine frailties and is comfortable with them and does not feel inferior on account of them. She takes them for granted and does not make any fuss about them. She likes reading a great deal and staying indoors. Thus she is essentially an indoor woman. But she marries an outdoor man without knowing it for him a small walk means ten miles. When they walk together, he walks too fast for her to catch up. After a little while, he looks back only to find her 200 yards behind. So she urges him to go ahead with his small walks while she remains indoors (pp 61-62). When their son is twelve, he goes along with his father for trekking while she stays home worrying about their safety as she imagines that bears may attack them on their way. She feels greatly relieved when they return safely with future plans for the next trek. She cannot help wondering if all the bears were hibernating this year, ready and waiting to come out in hordes next year !" (pp. 48). On another occasion, he leaves urgently to report to duty and she has to travel with the children and a great deal of luggage all alone. She accomplishes this challenging journey with great risk and difficulty (pp. 50-51). Dalal is not completely free from over - generalizations. While talking about writing middles, she remarks "On the whole, I fed the women writers capture the spirit of the middle more successfully than the men" Similarly, she over-generalizes her experience with the landlord in Hyderabad who never keeps his promise to get the necessary repairs done to the house. In her middle, "The Hyderabadi," she comments; "Of course the Hyderabadi hardly ever means what he says'.[15]

Dalal is impersonal in presenting and reporting the episodes and incidents; but she is not critical of them even when they result from our sexist culture. Once, she along with her friends attends a party. At the party, their host remarks that every man is a potential criminal. Then, all the guests unanimously express their disagreement. He, at once, asks a lady whether she will nod her head if this kills a mandarin in China and if it brings her good fortune. She replies that she will do it several times. He feels triumphant and says that nodding ones head and stabbing are one and the same if it is to kill a person. She protests and argues against his inference. Then, the discussion takes a new turn as another woman says that there are more men prisoners than women prisoners. Immediately, a senior police official retorts that it is because women use more subtle methods of killing a person than men. This leads to the altercation between the two opposite sexes. One woman points out that men kill people en masse in wars, and another young woman declares that men are essentially timid and awfully afraid of public opinion. The stormy discussion comes to an end with the final remark: "The gods did well to make me of a poor and timid spirit.'[16] The difference between men and women in their friendship as perceived by Dalal is presented well in "Those were the days". When old friends meet, men always feel nostalgic and remember their good old days. They spend a great deal of their time in talking about their past. But women never bother about their past. They are interested in the present. So they talk with great enthusiasm about the latest market prices, the latest trend in clothes and the iniquities of all servants. Finally, she remarks. "It is not that men utter any wise profundities when they are together -quite the contrary—but they so obviously enjoy being together".

Dalal's interest in plants and animals reveals her concern for fellow living organisms and environmental protection. She combines her scientific temperament and aesthetic sense as she describes the guava as a "Golden fruit" On the one hand, she is mindful of the Vitamin C content" (p.64), and urges her children to eat as many of them as possible; on the other hand, she describes its smell very romantically:

> It is a distinctive smell — not sharp like apples, nor lush and ripe like mangoes, but heavy and lingering, so that it curls like smoke in the corners of rooms, drifts around the doors and windows and comes to rest finally against the ceiling, where it seeps down filling the rooms with its stranges aroma.[18]

She, then, evokes a gut feeling in us for the fruit when she comments. "For my part I find a primitive satisfaction in seeing all this fruit, this embarrassment of nature's riches".[19]

In her middles on animals she expresses the same ambivalence attitude towards animals as she does in the case of men. "The Black Cat" exemplifies this. Once, a black cat enters her house. In exploring his new abode, he upsets many things and disturbs the people. Thus, he causes great annoyance to her. But her children treat him kindly and feed him well. So, he reciprocates their affection and wins their heart. She now cannot help loving him. She remarks:

> And now the black cat, the cold, the inscrutable, leaps eagerly into our arms and cries because he may not come for walks with us — and I, who did not particularly care for cats, find that he has, in some curious fashion, wound himself around my heart. [12]

Her other middles in which she writes lovingly about dogs, peacocks, and even pythons are equally interesting.

Dalal mocks at the wrong application of certain ideas by some people. Once, she comes across a Chinese proverb. 'If you have enough money for a loaf of bread, buy half a loaf and a rose " It impresses her so much that she at once starts feeling guilty of Catering only to the physical needs of the family instead of the aesthetic side" Then she decides: in future I should curtail the money spent for physical needs and nourish the spirit". So she buys a reproduction of a famous painting and gets it papered on the walls. Her children arrive from school and she expects them to appreciate her aesthetic endeavour. But, to her great disappointment, they do not show any interest in the painting. She consoles herself thinking that they are too young to understand the aesthetic value of the painting. So she waits for the adults to react. Later, the master arrives and feels horrified to see it. He tells her that people like them cannot afford to sacrifice half a loaf at all. Then she realizes: 'The Chinese proverb was quite obviously for an entirely different sort of family.'[22]

Dalal, as an ideal Indian lady, exhibits more tolerance and understanding than her husband. So he always finds fault with the modern fashions and the independent behaviour of their teen-age children. She has to function as a buffer between them. Finally, he having understood the inevitable gap between the generations, resigns himself to the current trends and fashions:

> He is constantly urging the teen-ager to look at me with my twenty-year-old hairstyle, my conventional make-up and my flat heels. Why can't you look like Mummy, "he says, a note of irritability creeping into his voice. I look with some trepidation at the slim, elegant young creature who is my daughter, but am instantly reassured, for on this point at least, she and her father agree entirely I look, it seems, the way a mother should look, in approval a smooth young check is pressed against mine and young arms go round me in quick hug".[23]

There are certain advantages of having a teen-age daughter and Dalal illustrates this in another middle. Her daughter grows into a charming young woman. Her parents gradually get used to the stares, the double-takes and the wolf-whistles that follow her progress down the road" (p 119). She, once, gets admitted in a big hospital for appendectomy. Her parents are really amazed to see her popularity. Even the doctors take more than professional interest in her. One of the doctors is a painter and wishes to show his paintings to her. And another doctor offers to give the best medical treatment. Dalal shrugs and says: There's one thing about having an attractive grown-up daughter around the house we meet the most curious assortment of people".[24]

Dalal does not write poetry – she never did. Yet her descriptions are often vivid and sometimes reach poetic heights. They are marked with accuracy and beauty. This makes reading her middles a rewarding and pleasurable experience. While describing a hill-station in Eagle's nest" for example, she writes:

> The moon shines white on the stone steps and silvers the trunks of the trees, throwing dark shadows under the rocks. Now and again a car hoots its way past on the road below, its headlights swinging by in an arc of light. The stillness is absolute, except the muffled beat of a distant drum.[25]

Talking about the disrupting effect of a puppy, she says:

> The disrupting effect on my ordered days is shattering. Never before have I watched so many sunrises. Every morning at an incredibly early hour I am out in the garden, half staggering with sleep, watching with weighted eyelids the rose-pink dawn creep over the sky, silhouetting the dark hills and dissipating the blue smoke from distant villages into the clear air while a small tan-and-white puppy gambols cheerfully on the grass.[26]

Dalal's other middles and her several articles and reports also share the same features as the middles. The gamut of themes covered in them reveal her versatile gifts (knowledge) wider knowledge, varied, interest, aesthetic sense and catholic views. This collection covers a variety of topics such as persons, places, plants, animals, literature, health and psychology. Tibet finds a good place in these articles. She describes

Tibetan culture with curiosity and zest especially the manner of selection of the Dalai Lama, the spiritual leader, she also draws attention to the problems caused by the communist government of China.

Thus, Dalal emerges as a versatile 'middle' writer for whom no topic is taboo, and who can create equal interest in a guava, a puppy, a bachelor, or a black cat! Indeed! There is never a dull moment reading her middles.

REFERENCES

1. Khushwant Singh, Introduction to Nergis Dalal's *Never a Dull Moment,* Calcutta: Orient Longmans, 1970, p. viii.
2. *Ibid,* p.vii.
3. Shatish Aikant in a letter to the author dated 09.01.1998.
4. K.V. Chacko preface, *Medley of Middles: A Collection of Essays,* Calcutta: Writers Workshop, 19.
5. Nergis Dalal, Introduction, *Never a Dull moment,* Calcutta, Orient Longmans, 1970, p.vii.
6. *Ibid.,* pp. vii-viii.
7. *Ibid.,* p. viii.
8. Nergis Dalal, *'Never a Dull Moment,* New Delhi, Orient Longmnan, 1970, p. 2.
9. .... "The Heart Remembers" *op. cit.,* p. 9.
10. .... "The Bachelor Friend" *op. cit.,* p. 4.
11. .... "Mario and the Indian Girls" *op. cit.,* p. 24.
12. .... "The Family Schneider", *op. cit.,* p. 66.
13. .... "The pen of my aunt", *op. cit.,* p.86.
14. .... "On writing middles", *op. cit.,* p.19.
15. .... "The Hyderabadi", *op. cit.,* p.75.
16. .... "A mandarin in China" *op. cit.,* p. 30.
17. Nergis Dalal, "Those were the days!", *op. it.,* p. 46.
18. .... "Golden fruit" *op. cit.,* p. 63.
19. .... *op. cit.,* p. 64.
20. .... "The black cat", *op. cit.,* p. 12.

21. .... "Half a loaf and a rose" *op. cit.*, p. 7.
22. *Ibid.*
23. Nergis Dalal, *"The terrible teens"*, *op. cit.*, p.112.
24. .... "Come and see my paintings!", *op. cit.*, p. 120.
25. .... "Eagle's next", *op. cit.*, p. 14.
26. .... "Puppy in the house", *op. cit.*, p. 25.

OTHER JOURNALISTIC WRITING

Nergis Dalal's other journalistic writings, which include hundreds of articles and book reviews published in leading national and regional newspapers remain relatively unknown. The articles cover a variety of themes, including her favourite topics like books, writers, women, yoga, the Dalai Lama, religion, meditation, health, environment, politics, social issues, etc. This chapter is an attempt to make known these relatively unknown writings of a creative writer who, as already suggested elsewhere in this study, has suffered critical inattention, in spite of her substantial output.

The Dalai Lama is obviously a favourite topic with her. She has not only published a number of articles on the Dalai Lama, but also reviewed a great many articles published as anthologies and books written by others about him. Through her articles on the Dalai Lama one can easily construct a rounded picture of this Buddhist monk, the spiritual leader of the world", who was forced to flee his country and live nearly 30 years in exile. Dalal feels he was the right choice for the Nobel Peace Prize for the Tibetans needed this award to help lighten the darkness of the days ahead", though it is difficult to see any light, however, in the tightening of Chinese restrictions..." she adds. Though "incurably optimistic", since the Lama hopes that "as we enter the 21st century ancient values that have sustained mankind will reaffirm themselves", "he is also perhaps the only Tibetan" according to Dalal "to see clearly, that the Nobel Prize, while honouring him for his consistent resistance to the use of violence in his people's struggle to regain their liberty, will ultimately make not an iota of difference to the reaction of the political world." (*Statesman*, 21 12.89).

The Dalai Lama knows well the bitter reality of his position and Dalal with her relentless enquiry tries to understand the contradictions that surround him in his exiled state.

Dalal, it appears, loves Tibet and the Tibetan Lamas, Tibetans, and the Tibetan way of life. In "The Tibet in India" published in *The Times of India* (25th September, 1988), she refers to their culture and their special traditions, talks about the great monasteries of Drepung, Sera and Ganden", destroyed in Tibet but recreated in Karnataka. Her interest and curiosity grow deeper as .... She talks about the Panchen Lama, Tenzen Tinlay, Jigime Choekyl, Wangechuk, the incarnation of lamas etc. The Tibetan way to "Healthy Life" impresses the reader with Dalal's knowledge of the Tibetan way of life. It is a scholarly article in which she writes about the traditional Tibetan art of healing at length, and of course, with her unfailing attention to the affairs of the Dalai Lama, she also writes about his personal physician, Dr. Tenzin Cheodhak.

Dalal is interested in everything. "Haiku Goes English" is about the Japanese three-part poem of usually 17 syllables" and how Haiku has become very much "a new English literary genre... "Hands up, Hijackers" tells how there are many practical courses on terrorism being conducted by experts at Universities, airports and defence institutes all over the world, which provide an insight into how terrorist operate their motives and preoccupations. "Write And Wrong" is about how writers and editors need each other. In "The Essential Reader" Dalal not only tells us why she reads – though for all kinds of reasons, primarily for entertainment and escape—but waxes poetic and quotes" to fade away, dissolve and quite forget, the weariness, the fever and the fret, here where men sit and hear each other groan". She lists the benefits of reading: "Those who read widely" she says, have a certain sophistication which makes them more open and tolerant of other peoples opinions, exposed as they are to such a wide spectrum of thought and minds. It leads us into new worlds of speculation which are necessary to understand the philosophical and other problems that confront us to-day.

She writes with a touch of humour, always bringing something of herself into her writing, even in this most objective kind of writing. She tells us how she has stacked her shelves with books on yoga, cookery, poetry, psychology literature and philosophy, and of course all those co-dependency books which I buy from time to time". She continues to tell us with her anecdotal style, how she was amused by "a New Yorker cartoon winch showed a man preparing to hang himself but in order to fit the noose around his neck, he is clambering up a pile of self-help books". Her punch is "I find these books fascinating although none of them have ever taught me how to cope with, cure or even control, the problems in my life" Another interesting instance quoted by her is about how her reading proved to be The most powerful sporific and tranquillizer" which succeeded in making the child in the hospital who was operated upon for appendicitis go to bed without any complaint.' In "Living with Books" she evinces her great love for books when she tells us:

> ... Books are a barrier against despair, a shield against the hazards of every day life, an open sesame into a magical world of the unknown where the normally tough if translucent membrane between the real and the imagined world is but a thin shifting veil. Despair, darkness and depression are better faced with books than with anything else. To be surrounded by books is, for a book lover, the ultimate delight.

"Talking of Women who write", Dalal has an important piece of advice for women: "Wouldn't they be better off, in the end more authentic, free and less pretentious", she says "If they used all their intelligence to find their proper place in the world. The proper place ordained by men?" She adds with her tongue in cheek.

It is with sheer delight that one reads her "Waiting for Godot". "Waiting for Godot" (the title of course is reminiscent of Beckett) is her waiting to be wiser, more circumspect, less credulous". The anecdotal quality of this article is simply wonderful. Her adventure, with borrowers of material for books or thesis they wish to write, is narrated with a lot of light-hearted gusto. She tells us about the Principal of the Special Training Institute (BCS) for IAS, IPS etc, who wrote "several pleading letters asking if he could use the whole of the first chapter from my books on yoga, for the English text book they were publishing, for, as he put it, the benefit of the student community and the youth of the state. I asked" she further says, "for a small payment for its inclusion in the book. After several letters in which he claimed they had no money, we finally settled for a one-time payment of Rs.750/ -. A ridiculously small sum, but I firmly believe that whatever is published, should be paid for."[9]

One year later, the Principal maintains that he is not in charge of payment and can do nothing about it. This makes Dalal fearlessly comment on the largely bleak picture" of the political and administrative climate of India.

Dalal is surprised and sad about the author of *Survival in Auschwitz.* Primo Levi who, having written something like this committed suicide. Dalal writes I am persuaded that normal human beings are biologically built for an activity that is aimed toward a goal, and that idleness or aimless work (like the meaningless work in Nazi prison camps) gives rise to suffering and to atrophy. In my case, work is identical with Problem solving, Primo Levi reached a stage in his life when he became so demoralised that he committed suicide". Dalal is disturbed, and she views the matter with empathetic, understanding, so much so that the reader too shares in equal measure her feeling for the tough man, who had managed to survive in "ruthless and oppressive" circumstances, but had always been aware of the mood of mourning and inconsolable despair and this, says Dalal, is perhaps the key to his tragic end.

Dalal, quite unmatched in her inspired choice of topics, writes even about maps! And even as she waxes a bit philosophical, she becomes matter-of-fact, which is an essential feature of her style:

> Maps are always fascinating and old maps even more so as we acknowledge how the *past continues to shape the present,* capturing and reflecting times past and defining the multiplicity of topographic and other changes. Hand-drawn and with clear and elegant lettering of place names, these maps are an indispensable source of information for the student, the historian and geographer, as well for the layman with an interest in maps (Emphasis added)

Dalal has something very interesting to say about diaries and diarists in her "Messages to an unconcerned world".

> "Diaries" according to her like most autobiographies, are best approached as a form of fiction, since diarists, while ostensibly writing for themselves; are in actual fact, waiting to contact the outside world, piling up their scattered impressions with an eye to publication".

Nobody could be more down-to-earth, clear-eyed in their objective expression of views than Dalal. She has a keen and inquiring mind. "Accent on Accent" a punning title, is about accents no doubt, but the development of the idea is intriguing. Her penchant for bringing in anecdotes is seen in almost all her journalistic articles. Here is an interesting example from "Accent On Accent"!

> I remember a young Dutch couple who were working in India on an assignment some years ago. Mrs H, looked just like a Dutch doll, with round pink cheeks, page-boy blonde hair and a fringe. Her English was fluent, but so heavily accented that it was sometimes impossible to understand. She was telling us the story of how she and her husband met, on board a ship, and neither knew the other was Dutch. He thought she was American, she thought he was English. "But couldn't you tell from your accents?" I asked puzzled. She looked both dismayed and astonished "I have an accent?" she asked. [13]

How absolutely amusing and at the same time serious are her articles "Do neurotic people make better writers?" Cross my Palm with Silver..." "A Writer confesses" open sesame" Personal dish antennas etc. She can, however, be quite serious at times as in "When I'm sixty-four", where she convincingly argues how prolonging life can be brutal and "how to die with dignity is as important as to live with dignity". She illustrates her argument with known examples, and pleads for an understanding of how important" it is to realize that Death can be seen as a welcome end to life, not something to be feared."

With her interest in Yoga and books on yoga, can she avoid writing about these things for the wide readership of newspapers. She has a number of articles on meditation, mind control, magic, myth, medicine etc. She feels, the greatest potential for improving the health of people can be created not by increasing the number of physicians but by motivating people to do things for themselves and their community". Dalal very boldly writes that "sickness caused by poorly-run hospitals, careless or badly trained doctors and outright malpractice can make medical treatment as much a threat as a cure in an article with a surprising title "Can Doctors Cause Diseases?"

Finally, Dalal defies categorization because of her amazingly wide range of interests, her keen observation, her knowledge, her scholarship, her ease at writing about anything from philosophy to pups, from kittens to traffic signals, from personalities to loud speakers, magic and travel. In these essay-like articles, she is naturally compact and lightly organized, and the style lacks the sparkle of poetic metaphors or the novelty of images. Dalal often flat and matter of fact. Nevertheless, one is impelled to read her, perhaps because what she says about Dhiren Bhagat in one of her journalistic articles may well be said about Dalal herself.

He had interesting, acute and sometimes unexpected things to say ... he had a restless mind, probing, enquiring, striving to comprehend; as much as possible.

("Dateline Destiny" *The Times of India*, 13.12.88)

REFERENCES

1. Nergis Dalal, "Nobel Prize Cannot Help Tibet" *Statesman*, 12th Dec, 1989.
2. ________, "Haiku Goes English", *Statesman* 18th July, 1987.
3. ________, "Hands up Hijackers", *Times of India*, 30th Sept,1984.
4. ________, "Write And Wrong", *Times of India*, 10th Jan, 1994.
5. ________, "The Essential Reader", *Times of India*, 7th May, 1993.
6. *Ibid.*
7. Nergis Dalal, "Living with Books", *Times of India*, 12th July, 1990
8. *Ibid.*
9. Nergis Dalal, *Pioneer*, 3rd Nov, 1997.
10. ________, "The Strange case of Primo Levi", *Statesman* 25th April, 1987.
11. ________, "Our past in maps", *Times of India*, 18th June, 1989.
12. ________, "Messages to an Unconcerned World", *Times of India*, 24th Dec, 1989.
13. ________, "Accent On Accent", *Times of India*, 17th June, 1989.
14. ________, "When I am Sixty Four", *Times of India*, 10th April, 1983.
15. ________, "Can Doctor's Cause Diseases?", *Indian Express*, 4th July, 1982.
16. ________, "Dateline Destiny", *Times of India*, 13th Dec, 1988.

7

Conclusion

Nergis Dalal is a writer who has contributed substantially to the world of letters. According to her:

> Writing creeps up insidiously — a compulsion to express ones innermost thoughts and feelings. A compulsion, as powerful and over-ruling as love or sex — to comment, to weave stories, to take a character and see where he is going.'

This only shows that she is creatively involved with society and seeks a full revelation in her works of what she finds in the world around her and within her. She earnestly feels that her active writing allows her to show the complexity of the world around her, the formidable forces that lie behind each explosive crisis and each dull dehumanizing routine, the limitations, dangers and excitements of a personal subjective view.

To date, she has produced four novels, a collection of short stories, hundreds of middles, and quite a few journalistic pieces. For each of her works, she gathers the material mostly from a distinctly Indian experience and weaves various threads into it from contemporary society. One observes a set pattern in all her works. Each of her works presents a slice of life, particularly a realistic account of the society around her.

Dalal's four novels deal with the theme of a search for meaningful existence in life. Her first novel *Minari is* about

Anita, the daughter of a retired General who, in the beginning is drawn towards the physical charm of Tejpore, an immoral person. In the end she realizes that Tejpore cannot provide her with the right emotional fulfillment. So, she returns to her husband's bedroom and thus reconciliation takes place with her realisation that she can find fulfillment only in her relationship with husband Ranjan.

Dalal's second novel *The Sisters* explores the attitudes towards marriage and human relationships through the changing perspective of Rita. The novelist examines, the contrasting marriages and attitudes to love of the ugly twin Rita' and the green-eyed beauty' Nina. The attitudes to marriage and love that unfurl in the novel represent the quest theme in this novel.

Dalal's third novel *The Inner Door* is about Rahul, who has lots of money and other material comforts. Yet, he doesn't conform to his expected social role of a wealthy guru in Rishikesh, and is not content with his status and wealth. The spiritual insights he recedes from the old Sadhu on the hills change his life. So, in the end he leaves his Ashram and searches for a new meaning in life.

Dalal's fourth novel *The Girls from Overseas* concentrates on the lives of foreign women married to Indian men. Widely separated by age and cultural differences, they are bound together by two factors — one, that all are foreigners and two, that their husbands are Indians. They are all prone to existential alienation. Despite their marriages to well placed professionals, they are unable to identity themselves with the Indian ethos. They become victims to their cultural disaffiliation. They cannot escape from their background. Their response to India is that of ethnocentrism, a tendency of all white people to judge others by their own values and beliefs. The novel markedly underlines Dalal's conviction that a dividing line separates the two cultures and can never be overcome. Naturally the girls experience an identity crisis, which intensifies their sense of despair. Thus, in the four novels one sees the running of thread of the theme of a quest for a identity a quest for meaning in life.

The theme of East-West encounter is undoubtedly a major concern of the Dalal canon. Westernized east has an aggressiveness about it as in the figures of Tejpore and Zora. This theme is more grippingly presented in *The Girls from Overseas* and in *The Inner Door*. The west emerges as an acquisitive materialistic force catering to raw passion in *The Inner Door*. The east, too, while preserving its traditional garb, is equally materialistic. The greed of Swamy Jagdish and Eashwari Devi and the latter's act of condoning Rahul's sexual relations are pointers in this direction. However, the east suggested in Rahul's transformation and in Duncan's becoming the first disciple is truly universal. Though sexual links of the girls to Jason and their attempts to preserve an alien identity are presented with compassion, the high point of the action is the unspoken rapport between Sandy and her mother-in-law Mataji. More importantly, the struggle of the girls to come to terms with India, mirrors a deeper struggle towards understanding themselves. Thus, the West's encounter with the East turns out to be one of the major concerns of the Dalal canon, though Dalal's East-West encounter theme does not match in depth (analysis) either that of Jhabvala or Kamala Markandaya.

Dalal's collection of short stories *The Nude* and her children's story *The Birthday Present* are taken up with different kinds of themes. In her Nude various themes pertaining to sex, unhappy marriage, the experience of women writers, delineate the characters who mostly search for meaning in life. The title story stands out among the collection with its theme of alienation. In fact, it mocks at the follies of civilization, which teaches us to enjoy the painting of a beautiful scene while ignoring the original beauty of Nature, as we get conditioned by culture, which begins to dictate our aesthete taste. Thus they indulge in various pleasures rather than enjoy the real ones. But creative artist, being free from the cultural dictates, perceives this and tries to make us understand it through his work.

The Birthday Present takes us into the world of child psychology. Dev's innate compassion forces him to choose an ill-treated ugly dog. Dev chooses Rajah, so that he can look after him and bring him round or rehabilitate him.

The world of Nergis Dalal is characterized by an element of passionate love for living creatures. Cruelty to animals is an unpardonable thing for her. Even worse is indifference to mongrels, pariah dogs and starving cattle. The mother in "A taste 'of Blood' is tormented by her husband weaning the child away from her. But it is the wanton shooting of birds which leads her to kill her husband. On the visit to Hardwar, Rita is appalled by the sight of man's indifference to cattle and dogs. Conversely monkeys eating out of Sunita's hand become a confirmation of her innocence and humanity. On many occasions, Dalal has commented directly on how the Indians abandoned their pet dogs to find for themselves. This recurrent note is perhaps attributable to the author's involvement with the society for the prevention of cruely to Animals.

Dalal's Middles' too record life in the society around her. The middles talk about the weaknesses, follies, foibles and the demerits of people. Dalal expresses her anger and then sympathizes with the follies of the people. She honestly admits her feminine frailties and laughs at them. In her Middles' one comes across various topics such as persons, places, plants, animals, literature, health and psychology.

They all describe various facets of life. The Middles's unfailingly lead the reader to perceive the silver lining. Life is livable in spite of problems, in spite of people. Dalal's journal articles introduce her as a very successful journalist. Her articles are crisp, informative and entertaining.

Again, her journalistic writings cover a wide variety of themes, particularly, themes pertaining to society. However, a few of Dalal's articles defy categorization. In the *Essential Reader*, she tells us of the many reasons for reading whatever she reads. She provides the reader with entrainment, but the same time, she would like to provoke him into thinking about life and its problems.

Nergis Dalal in her novels and short stories has employed various methods of narration. But she is quite at home with the method of the omniscient narrator as is evidenced in her novels as well as short stories.

An instance of the omniscient technique is as follows:

> The beautiful ones...they are handicapped from the beginning. Their beauty makes them neglect else—brain, heart, feelings. They are crippled emotionally —dangerous in their self-involvement. When they sleep with a man they see only themselves in his eyes. Always, they are watching themselves. No relationship with them can be anything but a failure. (*The Sisters*, p. 69)

Even in her short stories Dalal has employed the omniscient narrator technique. For example, in "The Intruder" she talks about the intruder thus:

> With sudden determination she went up and tugged furiously at the curtains. She tugged and tugged, shivering and numb with terror until at last they feel with a tearing rending sound, covering her completely. She began to struggle but the thick slippery material was everywhere. She tried to scream but something cold and fleshless closed around her throat. She felt herself sinking into a black bottomless pit. (*The Intruder*, p. 94)

Another sample may be taken from "The Silver Stallion".

> Against the thunder of his hooves the air rushed past. His legs moved with grace and precision and it was like watching the effortless flight of a bird, so smooth and swift was his passage. Only as an afterthought did they see the small figure flattened on the horse's back. (*The Silver Stallaion*, p. 83).

This method shows that the narrator tells everything about others as if he knows them inside out. Naturally, one perceive something unnatural and incredible in this method. It sounds unnatural on the part of the narrator to tell us everything about his different characters.

Dalal has employed the first person narrative technique also. This method allows the reader look deeply and analytically into the mind of a character. In fact, this narrative technique in her fiction allows us a peep into the mind or heart of the character, without letting self-directed look seem artificial. Here are a few examples.

> I fought back the tears that sprang into my eyes and put on my stubborn face. I would not show that I was hurt. All the foolish pleasure I had taken in my appearance vanished. The dress was absurd on me. I was fat, and the frills and flounces made me look like a small, stuffed pig. (*The Sisters*, p. 9)

Another instance of the first person narrative.

> From Nina's room upstairs I look out on the rose garden, the curved graveled drive that sweeps right around the house it is a beautiful house, my house. (*The Inner Door*, p. 6)

The first-person narration, as has already been pointed out, gives authenticity to the character in the story. Moreover, it endows the story with a realistic flavour. (The I' narrator significantly contributes to the development of the I' narrator's characters).

Nergis Dalal also employs flashback technique very

effectively. For example, in *The Sisters,* Rita reflects on her childhood. Here the past is unfurled. Sitting together, Rita and her sister recall their good old days. Questions and promptings by Nina lead Rita to recall the past. In the words of O.P. Bhatnagar:

> The technique of flashback and memories has been so intricately woven with the narrative in the present that it brings the whole drama of hurt feelings and irony with an intensity and compactness rare in the whole range of Indo - English Fiction[2].

Even in *The Girls from Overseas,* Dalal has tried the well-known flashback technique initiated by Henry James in English fiction of drawing characters away from their narrow securities and displacing them from their environment and studying their reactions.

One way through which verisimilitude can be achieved in literature is by using language realistically. But, it is also an undeniable fact that a certain amount of linguistic stylization becomes imperative in any literary creation. The sustained use of real language will not only hurt the aesthetic sense of the work but it will make the work unintelligible as well. The writer has to fashion his language into tool by means of which he can achieve verisimilitude in his work. Raja Rao says:

> We cannot write like the English. We should not. We cannot write only as Indians. We have grown to look at the large world as part of us. Our method of expression therefore, has to be a dialect which will some day prove to be as distinctive and colourful as the Irish or the American. Time alone will justify it".

If the Indian-English writer succeeds in fashioning a dialect of English as distinctively Indian as Raja Rao, for instance, does in his *Kanthapura,* he may be able to achieve verisimilitude to a considerable extent. But every Indian

English writer need not necessarily do so. Nergis Dalal comments on her own use of English in her works as follows:

> English is my native tongue, although my mother tongue is Gujarati. I was brought up in colonial times and like Nehru, I not only think in English, but dream in English as well.

In the Dalal canon there are mostly educated people knowing English quite well. They use their language quite consciously and look at the life of the common people with a certain amount of elitist detachment. The following samples show how easy it becomes for her to project Indian scenes and consciousness in a foreign medium:

> The once green face lay wounded, grimly bear. Without water, the crops withered and thousands of animals died. Somehow they had managed to save Moti. Even in that multitude of animals, Moti stood out a spectacularly beautiful horse, half thorough bred, half Kathiawar pony. His legs were clean and hard, he had a short strong back and broad forehead. His tail, high and glossy, rippled as he move. He was called Moti because he had the shimmer and colour of a pearl. (*The Silver Stallion,* p. 80)

Another important feature of Dalal's narrative mode is the way she depicts her emotional turmoil's in the lives of her characters. For example, Nina recounts her emotional insecurity thus:

> I wonder who coined that idiotic phrase about childhood, being the happiest days of our lives. Even thinking about it makes my stomach muscles tighten and shrink. As soon as I was aware that I was unhappy I began to build up around myself buffers to ease the ache .. I can remember with perfect clarity many scenes where it was necessary for me as a child to insulate myself from what was happening. I entered a dream world of my own, in which dimensions were blurred, and edges softened. It was the only way I could endure what was happening. (*The Sisters*, pp.119-120)

One is reminded of what O.P. Bhatnagar says about her,

bracketing her with writers like Kamala Markandaya, Malgaonkar, and Shantha Ram Rau:

> It is a happy augury for Indian fiction in English that a line of new novelists like Santha Rama Rau, Kamala Markandaya, Manohar Malgaonkar and Nergis Dalal are coming up to the fore who do not narrow down their art to any regional, religious or rural affiliations. They move about freely from nature to culture, village to town, poor to rich.... They write with perfect ease, grace and flexibility rendering credibility and finish to their creations.

Irony is one technique that Dalal employs in her works to great effect. The irony in the life of Anita is that Ranjan, an otherwise handsome and efficient young man, turns out to be dull as her husband. Rita is the worst victim of irony. The very sister from whom she had suffered crushing humiliations in childhood comes back to destroy her secure home which she had built with such emotional care. In *The Inner Door* while people invested million to make a fake saint out of Rahul, he turns out to be a real saint. Even her short stories exhibit ironies of life. Mr. Trianna of *'The Sacrifice'* who constigates India for its poverty, drought and famine is killed by the villagers and there are instant rains. Mr. Oliver, whose nude modeling with her delicate body and apricot skin had created one of the most sensational paintings of the times, fails to interest her husband, Mr. Oliver, in her baggy clothes. Even while he sees the replica of her nude painting at home he is driven out of home for the fulfillment of his desire. These twists and turns do not point towards a tragic view of life. Instead, they lead to a comic and light-hearted attitude towards life. Dalal is not committed to any particular philosophy or moral virtues but to the enrichment of life through a sensitive response. Her own sensitive response to life makes her pick up ordinary themes and turn them into aesthetic experience. Thus, one finds a constant use of irony in her art.

A word about the achievements of Dalal a creative writer. M.K. Naik is of the opinion that *Minari* sketches high-class life at a hill station with conventional characters in stock situations. Dr. S.D. Sharma on the contrary calls it an interesting novel that celebrates with poetic felicity the scenic grandeur of Minari. While Naik regards *The Sisters* as a failure, Bhatnagar sees in it Dalal's consummate mastery of description of scenes... memories and fantasies haunting the lonely self. While Naik finds fault with *The Inner Door* saying that the *Guide* motif of enforced sainthood is handled crudely, Bhatnagar is happy to juxtapose the implications of role-playing in Narayan's novel and Dalal's. While Naik dismisses *The Girls from Overseas* for treating insipidly the stock theme of East-West encounter, Bhatnagar sees in it, the first ever comprehensive study of foreigners in their intimate relationship with Indians in the country. According to Dr. Bhatnagar, this is the coolest and most objective of the East-West confrontations in family affairs. We may conclude that Nergis Dalal is a novelist writing in English with a facile pen. Her characters are both well developed and memorable and her novels are immensely readable. Her 'middles' and journalistic writings reveal to us her keen powers of observation and her ease at presenting a 'slice of life'.

However, in spite of it all she cannot rank with Anita Desai or even a Bharati Mukherjee, but it is difficult to put our finger on the exact reason why one feels she does not excite the reader as they do.

REFERENCES

1. "On How I Became a Writer", p. 9.
2. O.P. Bhatnagar, p. 138.
3. Raja Rao, Foreword to *Kanthapura*, Delhi, Orient Paperbacks, 1971, p. vi.
4. Questionnaire.
5. O.P. Bhatnagar, pp. 132-133.

Appendix

AN INTERVIEW

Q. *Why did you write novels? What do you want to tell your readers through your novels?*

A. I wrote novels in order to learn more about people and what makes them tick. Also because I like to tell stories. Someon once said that we write and read novels because we all like to look through the keyhole and find out what others are going or thinking.

Q. *Why did you switch over to the short story and what are the factors which motivated you to choose short stories?*

A. I did not 'switch over' to writing short stories. I wrote them long before I ever wrote a novel, and continued to write them at the same time as I wrote articles, novels and reviews.

Q. *Why did you not continue writing novels?*

A. For personal reasons.

Q. *In all your works the practice of yoga and women belonging to the upper-class are often reflected. Why?*

A. I write about the milieu to which I belong. Yoga has always been a passion of mine and therefore it makes its appearance in my writings.

Q. *Your writings are quite different from those of other women writers, why?*

A. This is the first time I have been told my writings are

different from those of other women writers. I should hope they were different from ALL other writers!

Q. *You are known mainly as a 'middle' writer why? What made you write middles?*

A. I wrote 'middles' before writing anything else. I must have written, by this time, literally hundreds and hundreds of middles. People seem to relate to them with warmth and affection. I have had more feedback from readers on my middles, than on any other form of writing.

Q. *Why did you adopt the pseudonym 'ARIES'? Why didn't you disclose your name?*

A. Because I was a very tentative writer and liked the cloak of anonymity.

Q. *In spite of writing novels, famous short stories, why are you not rated as a famous Indian woman writer in English?*

A. I do not think this is something I am qualified to answer. Luck perhaps, or Karma?

Q. *In your novels you often refer to military officials and their affairs with women, what is the reason?*

A. My husband was in the army and I used this as the background for some (certainly not all) of my novels.

Q. *Sex is the common factor in all your novels and other works. Why?*

A. I use sex very carefully in my novels and I certainly would not say it was central to my theme. In fact reviewers have often remarked that I display a puritanical streak, avoiding sex, and skirting around the issue.

Q. *In your middles North Eastern Hills people, religion and culture are repeatedly found. Why? What made you write on such topics?*

A. I write about what I am interested in, and what interests me more than anything else.

Q. What are your views on the writers of today?

A. Some are good, some are bad. My favourite women are P.D. James, Nadine Gordimer, Candia McWilliam, and Anita Brookner.

Q. Which is your favourite novel and why?

A. Currently I think my favourite novel is "The English Patient" by Michael Ondaatje. An exquisitely crafted love story and adventure story, combined with prose that is both descriptive and exceptionally beautiful. It is a novel that spans several worlds, told in a narrative that is both spare and imaginative. This is truly great novel.

Q. What is your attitude to the English Language as a medium of creative expression?

A. English is my native tongue, although my mother tongue is Gujarati. I was brought up in colonial times and like Nehru, I not only think in English, but dream in English as well.

Bibliography

I. PRIMARY SOURCES

NOVELS

Dala, Nergis *Minari*, Bombay: Pearl, 1967

______. *The Girls from Overseas*
New Delhi: Hind Pocket Books, 1979.

______. *The Inner Door*
New Delhi: Orient Longman, 1976.

______. *The Sisters,*
New Delhi: Hind Pocket Books, 1973.

SHORT STORIES

______. *The Nude*
New Delhi: Orient Paper Back, 1977.

______. *The Birthday Present*
New Delhi: Orient Paper Back, 1979 and 1997.

MIDDLES

______. Never a Dull Moment
New Delhi: Orient Longman, 1967.

YOGA

______. Yoga for Rejuvenation,
New Delhi: Orient Longman, 1992.

Index